Voodoo

Voodoo

New and future titles in the series include:

The Mystery Library

Voodoo

Stuart A. Kallen

LUCENT BOOKS

An imprint of Thomson Gale, a part of The Thomson Corporation

Detroit • New York • San Francisco • San Diego • New Haven, Conn. • Waterville, Maine • London • Munich

LIBRARY OF CONGRESS CATALOGING-IN-PUBLICATION DATA

Kallen, Stuart A., 1955–
    Voodoo / by Stuart A. Kallen.
        p. cm. — (Mystery library series)
    Includes bibliographical references and index.
    ISBN 1-59018-630-3 (hardcopy : alk. paper)
    1. Voodooism—Juvenile literature. I. Title. II. Series: Mystery library (Lucent Books)
    BL2490.K35 2005
    299.6'75—dc22

                                                            2004028213

Printed in the United States of America

Contents

Foreword

In Shakespeare's immortal play, *Hamlet*, the young Danish aristocrat Horatio has clearly been astonished and disconcerted by his encounter with a ghostlike apparition on the castle battlements. "There are more things in heaven and earth," his friend Hamlet assures him, "than are dreamt of in your philosophy."

Many people today would readily agree with Hamlet that the world and the vast universe surrounding it are teeming with wonders and oddities that remain largely outside the realm of present human knowledge or understanding. How did the universe begin? What caused the dinosaurs to become extinct? Was the lost continent of Atlantis a real place or merely legendary? Does a monstrous creature lurk beneath the surface of Scotland's Loch Ness? These are only a few of the intriguing questions that remain unanswered, despite the many great strides made by science in recent centuries.

Lucent Books' Mystery Library series is dedicated to exploring these and other perplexing, sometimes bizarre, and often disturbing or frightening wonders. Each volume in the series presents the best-known tales, incidents, and evidence surrounding the topic in question. Also included are the opinions and theories of scientists and other experts who have attempted to unravel and solve the ongoing mystery. And supplementing this information is a fulsome list of sources for further reading, providing the reader with the means to pursue the topic further.

The Mystery Library will satisfy every young reader's fascination for the unexplained. As one of history's greatest scientists, physicist Albert Einstein, put it:

> The most beautiful thing we can experience is the mysterious. It is the source of all true art and science. He to whom this emotion is a stranger, who can no longer wonder and stand rapt in awe, is as good as dead: his eyes are closed.

Introduction

The Many Sides of Voodoo

The word *voodoo* evokes many conflicting images. Fans of horror movies may envision ecstatic dancing, blood sacrifice, and wide-eyed zombies brought back from the dead. Those who believe in supernatural magic see voodoo as a means to cast spells for luck, love, money—or to be used in black magic to inflict pain and even death on enemies. For visitors to New Orleans, the self-described voodoo capital of the United States, voodoo may simply bring to mind bizarre shops in the French Quarter district where candles, incense, voodoo dolls, charms, and so-called magical potions are sold to tourists. For those who live in Haiti and elsewhere in the Caribbean, voodoo is a serious religion whose devotees can become possessed by the gods during intense ceremonies. For skeptics, voodoo is a colorful folk tradition, generally harmless despite seemingly inexplicable effects on what they consider unsophisticated believers. While the visions may differ, voodooism throughout the centuries has included all of these concepts and more. With an estimated 25 million believers throughout the world, voodoo means many things to many people.

Voodoo as a spiritual practice has its roots in the ancient beliefs of Africa and is named for *vodun*, which means "spirit" in the Fon language spoken in Benin and Nigeria in West Africa. In the French-speaking country of Haiti, where voodoo developed in the eighteenth century, the word is sometimes spelled vodou or vo-du. According to Haitian native Milo Rigaud in *Secrets of Voodoo*: "*Vo* means 'introspection' and *du* means 'into the unknown,'"[1] or a study of the unknown.

However it is spelled, voodoo is what is known as a syncretic practice. That is, it synthesizes or combines two belief systems into a unique doctrine. In voodoo the spirit worship

As part of a ritual, a voodoo priestess in New Orleans heats the tip of a spear with a candle. Voodoo has its roots in ancient African beliefs.

11

of ancient Africa is blended with elements of Roman Catholicism, especially the veneration of saints. For this reason, there is a saying in Haiti that "ninety percent of the people [are] Catholic and one hundred percent voodoo."[2] Some argue, however, that voodoo is not a religion at all, according to Phyllis Galembo in *Vodou*:

> It has been said that Vodou is not a religion but a practice: This is not to downplay the spiritual importance of the tradition, but to emphasize the importance of active service rather than passive belief in Vodou spirituality. Followers of Vodou do not identify themselves as "Vodouists," as adherents of the Catholic church would say they are "Catholics." Rather they say they are "servants of the spirits."[3]

Ridden by the Loas

Believers in voodoo say that a single god created heaven and earth. This god has several names. He is known as *Mawu-Lisa* or *Olorun* in West Africa and *Gran Mèt* (Great Master) or *Bondyé* in Haiti. Too powerful and magnificent to bother with the mundane daily desires of human beings, *Gran Mèt* created hundreds of spirits to act as his intermediaries on earth. These spirits, called *loa, loas, lwas,* or *mystères* —French for "mysteries"—are said to rule many vital forces of life. For example, the deity Azacca is the loa of agriculture, Bade is the loa of wind, and Simbi is guardian of the fountains, marshes, and bodies of freshwater. Other deities represent human concerns such as war, love, death, and even apathy. (The loa are said to be spirits; supernatural beings related to various functions of the universe such as agriculture, death, and so on. However, they are oftentimes referred to as gods, goddesses, or deities by writers and voodoo practitioners.)

Voodooists consult with the loas before they engage in any important activities such as marriage, moving, opening a

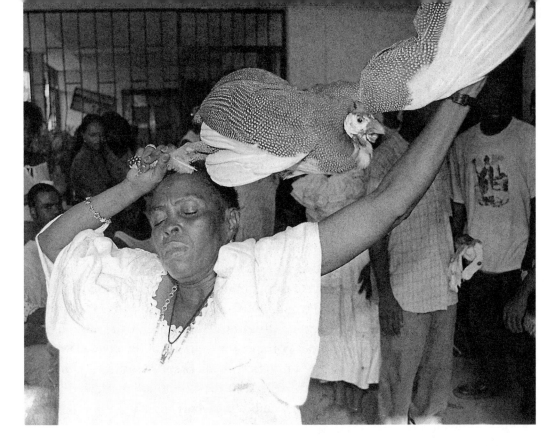

business, or planting crops. To do so, they pray, sing, play drums, and dance until they enter a hypnotic state known as a possession trance. During this activity, the loa are said to enter, or possess, the bodies of the voodooists and "ride" them like "horses." For this reason, voodooists refer to spirit possession as being ridden as a spirit horse. These loas are able to magically influence the lives of devotees in many positive ways, as Samuel H. Williams writes in *Voodoo Roads*:

A Haitian woman in a voodoo trance waves a guinea fowl over her head. Voodoo is recognized as an official religion in Haiti.

> Voodooism . . . is a code of living in which the natives use the [loas] to cure sickness, drive away evil forces, stimulate effort, modify behaviour, and secure a livelihood. It has the same effect upon people who practice it that prayer has upon a Christian; it stimulates endeavor and [soothes] a troubled mind. In it are incorporated the ideas of faith, autosuggestion, and fear, all of which are potent factors in making any religion function.[4]

For many Haitians, voodoo is the only hope in a troubled land where 75 percent of the people are unemployed and where drug gangs, antigovernment rebels, and common criminals create a climate of fear and violence. To the multitudes who often go hungry and lack basic necessities such as running water, electricity, and sewage treatment, possession by voodoo loas is the only respite from daily life in the poorest nation in the Western Hemisphere.

While some see voodoo as nothing more than superstition, to believers throughout the world, it represents a complex and ancient tradition rooted in Africa. With its frenetic dancing, energetic drumming, and spectacular ceremonies, voodoo provides comfort for millions of devotees. Whether it is a religion, a practice, or, as skeptics say, a folkloric superstition, matters little to those who are possessed by the loas and taken to a land of heavenly delights.

Chapter 1

Historic Roots

Voodoo is folk religion that evolved among African people during a time of crisis. In the eighteenth century more than a half million men, women, and children from West African ethnic groups such as the Ibo, Dahomey, Congo, Ewe, and Susu were kidnapped in their homelands and sent to French plantations on the island of Haiti in the Caribbean. As historian Ron Bodin writes in *Voodoo Past and Present*: "Slave ships, floating hellholes, scooped up an angry, confused, unwilling human cargo from the African continent and transported a proud people to a life of servitude in the New World."[5] Although these Africans had many cultural differences—and spoke different languages—they held common spiritual convictions that were very different from those of their captors, most of whom were Christians.

In the traditional view of the West Africans, human beings inhabit a world that is rife with spirits of nature and the dead. These spirits can control the destinies of people in positive and negative ways. For example, spirits of the rain and clouds can provide life-giving waters—or cause starvation-inducing droughts. Spirits of animals can bequeath wisdom and strength upon humans—or bring bad luck through evil spells. Spirits of ancestors can watch over and protect a person—or block his or her path to happiness. Historian Jim

Haskins explains the characteristics of the African spirits in *Voodoo and Hoodoo*:

> The soil, the rocks and mountains, the trees, the rivers are all believed to be inhabited by spirits— spirits that never knew human form. They share spirit-space with the ghosts of departed ancestors. The latter continue to affect the lives of their offspring, positively or negatively, depending on how they were treated when alive. And they exercise as tangible an effect as do the spirits of natural phenomena.[6]

While human beings may be influenced by the spirits of nature and the dead, it is believed that people can also peti-

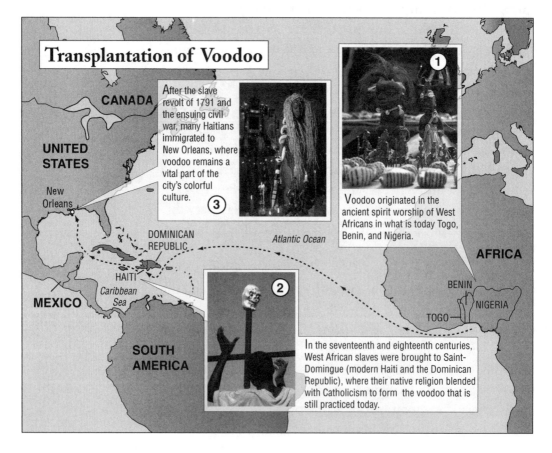

Transplantation of Voodoo

After the slave revolt of 1791 and the ensuing civil war, many Haitians immigrated to New Orleans, where voodoo remains a vital part of the city's colorful culture. ③

Voodoo originated in the ancient spirit worship of West Africans in what is today Togo, Benin, and Nigeria.

In the seventeenth and eighteenth centuries, West African slaves were brought to Saint-Domingue (modern Haiti and the Dominican Republic), where their native religion blended with Catholicism to form the voodoo that is still practiced today.

tion, or negotiate with, these forces through magic spells and ceremonial songs and dances. For example, a healer, or medicine man, might try to cure a sick person by reciting magical chants or drumming and dancing for hours to channel the help of the deities. Conversely, a magician or conjurer with evil intent could petition the spirits to cause an enemy distress, physical ailments, or even death. Because of these powers, Bodin writes, "man needed to know about the gods to protect himself from spiritual or catastrophic harm."[7]

Belief in spirits was a central part of life for West Africans. They could not escape the harsh reality of slavery, however, when French slave traders invaded their shores and brutally separated thousands of people from their friends, family, villages, and culture. Many were average citizens, but others were priests, sorcerers, and tribal chiefs. These people were deeply involved with spirit magic, religious rites, and ancient tribal customs. While they were forced to leave their homeland behind, the religious specialists transported a form of voodoo from Africa to Saint-Domingue. This island, now called Hispaniola, is shared today by Haiti and the Dominican Republic.

"Bizarre Practices"

The slaves in Saint-Domingue came from many regions. However, they were primarily from Dahomey—an area that included parts of present-day Nigeria, Benin, and Togo. According to anthropologist Alfred Mêtraux in *Voodoo in Haiti*, the Dahomean priests who were among the slaves "contrived to resurrect, in exile, the religious framework in which they had been brought up. *[Boko]* (magicians) and *vodû-no* (priests), [who had been] trained in Africa, taught the following generations, born in slavery, the names and characteristics of the gods and the sacrifices required."[8]

The traditional African religion provided the slaves with some amount of strength and comfort as they worked under

Keeping Ancient Traditions Alive

Plantation slaves in Saint-Domingue were often forced to work more than sixteen hours a day and many were worked to death. Despite the hardships, they kept their ancient voodoo traditions alive, as Alfred Mêtraux explains in *Voodoo in Haiti*:

Slavery could have demoralized [practitioners of voodoo] completely and sunk them into that gloomy apathy which goes with servitude. Mere physical exhaustion should have prevented them from dancing and singing as Voodoo ritual requires. Apart from the cruelties of which they were the helpless victims, slaves were made to work, even by good owners, to the limit of human capacity. "For the Negroes work starts before dawn"—wrote Girod-Chantrans in 1782. "At eight o'clock they get their dinner; they go back to work till midday. At two o'clock they start again and carry on till nightfall; sometimes right up to ten or eleven p.m." The two hours allowed in the middle of the day, and all holidays, were given over to the cultivation of their own foodstuffs. . . . The over-exertion was so crushing that the life of a Negro sold to a plantation in Saint-Domingue was reckoned at never more than ten years. We can but admire the devotion of those slaves who sacrificed their rest and their sleep to resurrect the religions of their tribes . . . in the most precarious conditions.

barbaric conditions in distilleries and tanneries, and on sugar, cotton, and coffee plantations. The religion was also a way to rebel, to possess their own spirituality, in a system in which they were allowed to own nothing.

It took courage to believe in voodoo because it was considered satanic by the French slave owners, who passed laws to prevent its practice. Since dancing plays a central role in voodoo ceremonies, an ordinance passed in 1704 specifically prevented "gathering at night under the pretext of holding collective dances."[9] This decree must have been widely ignored because in 1765 a small military unit, the First Legion of Saint-Domingue, was formed with the specific purpose of breaking up the forbidden night dances.

Despite the efforts of the authorities, the black people of Saint-Domingue were able to practice their African-based religion. While they often kept their ceremonies secret, occasionally they would allow a sympathetic white person to attend. In 1797, one such observer, French writer M.L.E. Moreau de Saint-Mery, wrote the first detailed description of voodoo and its rituals.

Moreau de Saint-Mery states that voodoo is not only an African dance but also an institution "in which superstition and some bizarre practices have a great part."[10] The author says that the central voodoo god, Gran Mèt, is "an all-powerful, supernatural being. Upon this being hang all the events which occur on this globe."[11] Moreau de Saint-Mery describes a voodoo ceremony, writing that those in attendance are sworn to secrecy after which a snake, representing Gran Mèt, is glorified by the crowd. Those assembled are then allowed to ask the voodoo gods to grant their wishes:

> Most slaves ask for the ability to direct the thoughts of their masters. But this is not enough. One begs for money. Another seeks the gift of pleasing a girl who will pay no attention to him. This one wishes to call back an unfaithful mistress, that one asks to be made well or to have a longer life. After them, an old woman wants to implore God to stop the scorn of someone whose happy youth she would capture. A young girl asks for everlasting love—or repeats the wishes that hatred dictates to her as to a preferred rival.[12]

These invocations are followed by frenzied dancing to the rhythmic sounds of drums and hand claps. Dancers spin around and around until they go into a trance, causing them to faint or experience rapture. At dawn the ceremony ends. The experience frightened Moreau de Saint-Mery, however. Like many among the white minority on Haiti, he feared that voodoo gave too much power to the slaves: "Nothing is more dangerous," he wrote, " . . . than this cult of Voodoo. It can be made into a terrible weapon."[13]

The Holy and Profane

Moreau de Saint-Mery seemed unaware that practitioners of voodoo took some of their inspiration from Christianity. According to a 1665 decree, the slaves of Saint-Domingue were required to "be baptized and instructed in the Catholic, Apostolic, and Roman religion." Those who bought newly arrived Africans had to "give the necessary orders for the baptism and instruction of the slaves."[14]

Despite this decree, most plantation owners did not teach Catholicism to their slaves. Most were content to simply sprinkle their workers with a little holy water before sending them to toil in the fields. Others drove their slaves into church with whips and forced them to kneel as a priest baptized them as a group. There were, however, opportunities for some slaves to become more familiar with Catholic teachings. For example, slaves who were cooks, gardeners, maids, butlers, and stable hands worked on plantation grounds and in their masters' homes. These so-called house slaves often prayed and read the Bible with white families at night and attended Mass on Sundays. There were also thousands of free blacks who attended church and practiced the dominant religion of the powerful whites who ruled the island. In addition, Jesuit missionaries traveled to Saint-Domingue with the specific purpose of Christianizing all slaves.

When those of African descent learned Christian teachings, they were able to place voodoo spirit deities and Catholic saints side by side. Haskins provides several examples:

> [In Haiti] where many of the slaves were of Dahomean heritage, the Dahomean serpent-deity Da was identified with Saint Patrick [who was said to have driven the snakes out of Ireland]. The Dahomean [deity] Legba, guard of entrances and god

of the crossroads, was identified with Saint Peter, the keeper of the keys [to the Kingdom of Heaven].[15]

This sixteenth-century engraving shows African slaves at work on a sugar plantation in Haiti. French slave owners tried to stamp out voodoo practices.

The connections and comparisons between the Catholic saints and the African pantheon, or group of gods, were probably first made by Dahomean priests, medicine men, and sorcerers. These people undoubtedly discovered that they could continue practicing their ancient religion without punishment if they used the symbolism of the Catholic Church to express voodoo beliefs. Thus when they performed spells, magical charms and amulets were deployed in conjunction with the cross. In 1761 a decree by the *Conseil du Cap*, or Council of Cape, complained about these practices. Although the slaves in the town of Cape were trained by Jesuits as churchwardens and choir conductors, they only "pretended to copy the practices of a Church Council . . . [and they] often mingled the Holy utensils of our religion with profane and idolatrous objects . . . and thus

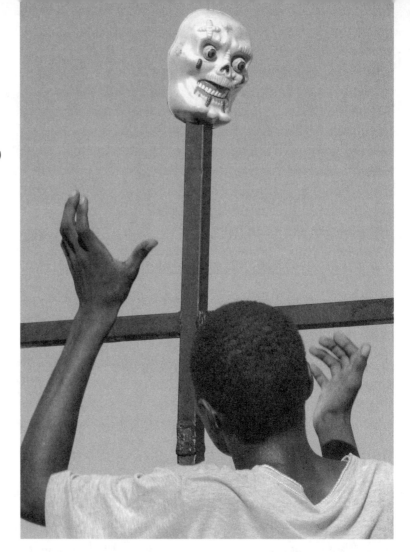

As part of a ceremony to honor an ancestor, a Haitian man has placed a skull (a voodoo symbol) on top of a cross (a Christian symbol).

the truths and the dogmas of religion were altered."[16] A Catholic priest, Father Labat, put it even more bluntly in 1722, writing, "The Negroes have no scruples. They . . . secretly keep all the superstitions of their ancient idolatrous cult alongside the ceremonies of the Christian religion."[17]

Destruction and Deliverance

The mixing of voodoo and Catholicism was alarming to the French on Saint-Domingue, where slaves outnumbered whites by a ratio of eleven to one. Planters and government officials feared that the unique religion empowered the slaves and might lead to an insurrection. For this reason, those who were caught practicing voodoo were dealt swift and ruthless punishment. According to Rigaud: "Slaves found in possession of any symbol of Voodoo were punished with lashings, imprisonments, hangings, and 'blanchings' [stripping the skin off a disobedient slave until the white tissue was exposed]."[18] Other punishments included burying a voodoo practitioner up to his neck in sand and pouring molasses over his head to attract bees, ants, and flies. Slaves were also mutilated in horrible ways, branded with hot irons, or even thrown live into huge baking ovens.

Instead of quelling slave revolts, such atrocities only encouraged rebellion. On August 14, 1791, an insurrection led by a slave named Boukman began at a voodoo ceremony where a large number of slaves had gathered to drum and dance in a forest. As the evening progressed, a torrential

A Melding of Beliefs

The voodoo culture of eighteenth-century Haiti blended African spirit worship and French Catholicism. In *Voodoo and Hoodoo* Jim Haskins describes the similarities of the two belief systems and explains why slaves were able to meld the two:

[The] people of Dahomey and Yoruba, who were most numerous in [Haiti], were also the slaves whose religion was characterized by a highly developed pantheon [group of gods].

The Catholic Church had a pantheon of its own. Its Virgin [Mary] and its saints were understandable to Africans whose religious structure and traditions included lesser but important deities who were, like the saints, honored with festivals and rituals and prayed to for help

in day-to-day living. Christianity even included a Devil, [an evil] spirit with whom the Africans could easily find parallels. The Catholic religion was also highly ritualistic; its Holy Communion, holy days, and its services could correspond in the African's mind to his own rituals, its rosary beads and icons to his talismans [magical charms]. And not only did the equation exist, it was encouraged. The Church decreed missionary work among the slaves. Conversion to Catholicism, ideally in its pure form, was wanted, but given the "primitive" and "heathenish" background of the slaves [according to church leaders], certain adulterations of the practice of the faith were overlooked in the process of bringing new souls to God.

rainstorm with intense thunder and lightning whipped tree branches through the air. In the midst of this dramatic scene, an aged voodoo priestess rose up to sing while waving a huge cutlass over her head. According to a legendary account taught to all Haitian schoolchildren in the nineteenth century:

> At this moment a black pig is produced. The din of the storm drowns his grunts. With one vivid thrust the inspired priestess plunges her cutlass into the animal's throat. The blood spurts—and is gathered smoking to be distributed in turn, to the slaves; all drink, all swear to obey Boukman.[19]

This illustration depicts the slave revolt of 1791. The revolt marked the beginning of a long civil war that resulted in a rebel victory and independence for Haiti.

The crowd, energized by the supernatural scene, invaded Bois Caiman, a town on the northern part of the island, indiscriminately killing white men, women, and children. In the days that followed, the scene was repeated in other towns and villages as more than six thousand slaves burned more than a thousand plantations.

While Boukman was soon caught and decapitated, the slave revolt of 1791 was the beginning of a voodoo-inspired civil war that continued for the next thirteen years. The rebel army was made up of two factions: Africans who still practiced their indigenous religion unmixed with any elements of Christianity and voodooists from Haiti. The rebels eventually prevailed, and on January 1, 1804, the half million blacks on Saint-Domingue finally put an end to French rule. The victors named the first independent black nation Haiti, an Indian word meaning "mountainous country."

The success of the rebel generals during the bloody revolution has been directly attributed to voodoo prayers, spells, and magical rites. As historian Dantès Bellegarde writes, "The slaves found in Voodoo the ideal stimulus for their energy—since Voodoo had become less a religion than a political association . . . dedicated to the destruction of the Whites and the deliverance of the Negroes."[20] This historic revolution would also affect the nation's dominant religion. Catholic priests fled the country, leaving most rural churches with no clergy. As Mêtraux writes:

> With the Revolution . . . a new chapter in the history of Voodoo opens. Gone are the ties with Africa, the Catholic clergy is scattered and official control of religious activity is no longer so strict. Voodoo can evolve freely, sealed off [on an island from the rest of the world], receiving [only small] contributions . . . from Catholicism.[21]

Bonfires Blazed in New Orleans

Although Haiti became an independent nation after the revolution, no other country in the world would recognize its independence. Former trading partners, such as the United States, cut off relations with Haiti, fearing the slave revolt might spread to U.S. shores where slavery was still legal. In the years that followed, poverty and political violence increased until Haiti was the poorest nation in the Western Hemisphere, a distinction it would hold into the twenty-first century.

As Haiti sank into chaos, many blacks fled the island. About ten thousand made their way to the United States, with most of them settling in New Orleans, which had been acquired from France as part of the Louisiana Purchase of 1803. The city, known as the Paris of America, was one of the most multicultural in North America, with African slaves, immigrants from the Caribbean, Europeans, Americans, and free light-skinned blacks called Creoles all living, working, and playing together. Although most residents were devout Catholics, the city had long had a voodoo influence as a result of French trade with Saint-Domingue. With the influx of Haitians, voodoo became an important element in New Orleans culture.

Slaves line up to be auctioned in New Orleans in this sketch. After Haiti achieved independence, thousands of blacks came to New Orleans.

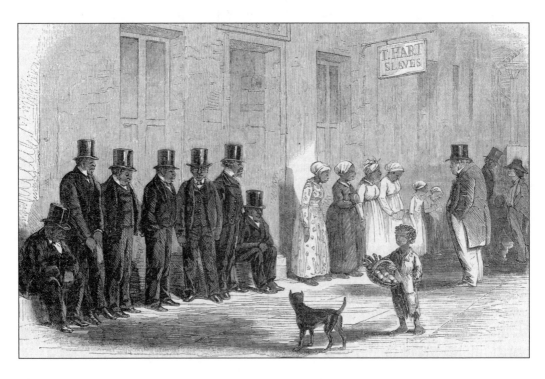

Although slavery was legal in New Orleans, slaves were not treated as brutally as those in Haiti and elsewhere in the American South. On Sundays, many slaves attended church and were allowed to take the afternoon off. In the early 1800s, slaves and free blacks would gather in Congo Square, a small park in the heart of New Orleans, to play drums and perform traditional African dances. It was a place reserved by authorities for the free expression of African culture, where voodoo charms were sold and voodoo ceremonies held. These dances, however, were not the orgiastic, frenzied rituals of genuine voodoo ceremony but cleaned-up versions put on for tourists, as Robert Tallant writes in *Voodoo in New Orleans*:

> [While] the white people gaped . . . they performed the Calinda and the Bamboula and other dances of a relatively mild character, omitting the more grotesque and sensual features of [traditional voodoo ceremonies], and they wore not their red loincloths, ankle bells and knee rings, but all the castoff finery they had been able to coax from their masters and mistresses. Sometimes they did attach metal rattlers to their legs, and this and the Congo drums always in use were the only music needed. . . . They did sing the Voodoo songs, but most of these the white public could not understand—even when they were mocking the whites —and it considered them . . . harmless.[22]

Such gatherings attracted people from across all echelons of New Orleans society, including wealthy white women. The spectacle of these uninhibited women dancing wildly in public fueled hundreds of sensationalistic newspaper stories. During the 1820s, newspapers, politicians, and religious leaders waged a fierce anti-voodoo campaign. By the end of the 1830s, laws were passed that banned dancing on Congo Square. This only served to

A crowd watches as a man performs a voodoo dance with a plate of hot coals on his head. Such public spectacles rarely incorporated genuine voodoo elements.

drive the voodoo underground. As in Saint-Domingue, voodoo rites continued in secret, usually in dense glades on the shores of nearby Lake Pontchartrain. As Tallant writes: "Here the bonfires blazed and the drums took up their beat. Here were the snake and the sacrifice and the bowl of blood."[23]

Dr. John the Root Doctor

Despite the secretive nature of voodoo, there were a few men and women who became famous for their alleged voodoo powers. These people used herbs and spells—and often blatant self-promotion—to get rich. Along the way, they helped make voodoo more acceptable among the general population.

In the 1840s, one of the most important voodoo figures was an ex-slave known as Dr. John, John Bayou, or John

Montenet, who claimed to have once been an African prince in Senegal. While working on the docks in New Orleans, Dr. John decided that he had special powers, which he soon used to declare himself a voodoo priest or "root doctor." Thereafter, clients paid him to predict the future, read minds, cast spells, make magical herbal potions, and remove curses. While skeptics doubted his powers, his clients showered him with money and gifts. He used his money to build a house that he filled with snakes, lizards, embalmed scorpions, and human skulls allegedly pilfered from local graveyards. Dr. John also bought fifteen female slaves with whom he purportedly had fifty children. Tallant describes the activities of the voodoo doctor:

> To his cottage came thousands. He placed and lifted curses for a fee. He combined pseudomedical practices, astrology and divination with [allegedly magical] pebbles. Fine white ladies, heavily veiled, sought his advice regarding their love affairs and bought a tiny bottle [of magic potion] from him for a fabulous price. Many a young beau and aging [gentleman] paid a large sum for a shell wrapped in a twist of human hair or a packet of [magical] powder, to be used in winning the favor of some girl, perhaps white and rich and acceptable socially, perhaps [black] and beautiful and desirable. Parents sought his aid for the protection of wayward sons or daughters. Sick people sought health, and old men and women sought youth. There were, too, those who paid him regular sums through sheer terror of some secret knowledge that he held.[24]

Dr. John did possess secrets, but they often had little to do with voodoo magic. Instead, the root doctor consulted with dozens of black servants who worked in the best homes in New Orleans. This army of paid informers reported back to Dr. John with news of love affairs, secret trysts, marital difficulties, bad business deals, and other overheard gossip. When wealthy white clients drove their fine carriages to the doctor's seemingly haunted house, the ex-slave with a tattooed face calmly related back to them intimate details of their lives. For a fee, the doctor offered to read their minds and give advice. For a larger sum, he offered to keep their dealings secret so that they would not be ruined.

The Voodoo Queen of New Orleans

Dr. John had a female counterpart named Marie Laveau. Born in 1794, Laveau was a free woman of color, known in the parlance of the time as a quadroon—a person with one black grandparent. She began her career as a hairdresser, working in the homes of affluent white women. Like Dr. John's informers, Laveau heard quite a bit about love affairs as she rearranged the tresses of society's most privileged women. This knowledge enabled her to become a voodoo priestess, according to Lindsey Tubbs and Esther Liu on Parascope's "Marie Laveau" Web page:

> By hearing all the gossip in her salon that the white women freely let fall from their lips, Laveau learned many secrets and such, which enabled her to "foresee the future" or tell her clients what was really going on using her "powers." Through this gossip, Laveau was able to build up a network of informers. These spies were used to "cure" the cheating husbands of her clients, or more likely blackmail the mistresses of the cheating husbands.[25]

Using her ruthless business sense and trading on her good looks and theatrical flair, Laveau was the undisputed voodoo queen of New Orleans by the 1830s. Like Dr. John, she charged large sums for her services. She shrewdly avoided persecution by anti-voodoo authorities by further

Christianizing voodoo, "adding to traditional voodoo paraphernalia statues of Catholic saints, prayers, incense, candles, and holy water,"[26] according to Haskins.

With her wealth and powers, Laveau herself was treated as a saint by New Orleans residents, and she was often called the Queen of the Saints. Insisting that voodoo practitioners were good Christians, Laveau practiced her trade in the open. She invited politicians, the police, the press, and influential white citizens to observe voodoo rituals. These were sanitized ceremonies, but they greatly increased her business. Laveau also attracted great attention performing her sensual voodoo snake dance at Sunday gatherings at Congo Square. An ex-slave, Tom Bragg, described the scene:

The Snake Dance

Marie Laveau was a legendary voodoo queen in New Orleans. She was the first to cast voodoo spells for a fee and she enhanced her reputation by performing voodoo dances on Sundays in Congo Square. In *Voodoo Queen: The Spirited Lives of Marie Laveau*, Martha Ward describes Laveau's snake dance:

Marie slipped off her shoes and walked to the center [of Congo Square] where magical lines from the four corners and the four gates intersected. As was her custom, she knelt on the ground and rapped three times. The crowd loved the one-two-three rhythm [of her magic chant] and shouted it with her—Father, Son, and Holy Ghost. Faith, Hope, and Charity. Then from a box near her feet, she lifted a fat snake. The earth-toned creature—probably a Louisiana [boa constrictor]—was not poisonous, but it stretched twelve to twenty feet and entwined itself in undulating coils about the body of the priestess. . . . Marie signaled the band and began to move with slow, sinuous grace. Bare soles flat on the packed earth of Congo Square, she shifted her weight from one ankle to another, then to her knees, thighs, hips, torso, and up to her shoulders. Her feet never lifted from the ground; she swayed in waves like the movement of snakes. Other women joined her and danced within their own tight circles or rings, some no larger than ten feet in diameter. Many waved white handkerchiefs. . . . Men with bracelets of bells on their calves danced in circles around the women. Sometimes they balanced bottles of rum or other spirits on their heads. They mimicked fighting and leaped into the air in displays of gymnastic ferocity.

Tourists pose for a photo at the tomb of Marie Laveau, New Orleans's most famous voodoo queen.

"When she got through dancin' . . . she could make anybody do anything and sometimes she made 'em do terrible things. She made people disappear. She made wives turn on their husbands and run off wit' other men. She made fine white ladies lie on the ground and roll on their bellies."[27]

Like many stories about voodoo, Bragg's may be greatly exaggerated. Nevertheless, voodoo, with its sensuous secret ceremonies and entertaining but more sedate public spectacles, became an integral part of New Orleans society. Sometime after the 1860s, it came to be known as hoodoo by some, although that term technically means a charm or amulet. Today about 15 percent of the city's population claims to practice voodoo, while thousands of tourists travel to New Orleans to visit voodoo and hoodoo shops in the French Quarter and visit Marie Laveau's grave in St. Louis Cemetery.

In Haiti, voodoo remains an important part of daily life for many of the citizens of that long-suffering nation. Although the rites and rituals of voodoo have changed little over the past several centuries, voodooists no longer have to practice their beliefs in secret. To them, voodoo is more than a colorful oddity of history. Instead it is a serious belief that they can turn to in times of need.

Chapter 2

Houngan, Mambos, and Rituals

Those who practice voodoo use rituals to make contact with loa, also known as the *mystères* or mysterious spirits. The loa are contacted before and after life-changing events such as marriage, birth, and recovery from serious illness. Rituals are also held to shake off a run of bad luck, when a person falls ill, or after someone dies. In addition, there are dozens of voodoo holidays, up to four or five per month, that honor different loa, celebrate the change of seasons, or remember ancestors.

Unlike ceremonies performed by mainstream religions, which are often the same year after year, voodoo rituals are improvised so that no two are exactly alike. Most have similar components, however. For example, the earliest known description of a voodoo ceremony, written in 1797 by French scholar M.L.E. Moreau de Saint-Mery, shows many similarities to rituals that take place today in Haiti. The eighteenth-century ritual was conducted by a voodoo king or priest, known as papa-loa, or *houngan* (also spelled *hungan* or *houn'gan*). Central to the ritual was a voodoo queen or priestess, known as mama-loa, *mambo*, or *mam'bo*. The houngan and mambo presided over a ritual held at a voodoo temple, called a *hounfour* or *humfort*. The rite was attended by dozens of slaves, free people of color, and a few white observers such as Moreau de Saint-Mery.

A Rite That Has Scarcely Changed

The ceremony began with the entrance of the king and queen, who wore outfits made only of red handkerchiefs tied together. The ritual was held to initiate new members to the

A priestess in New Orleans performs a voodoo ceremony with a snake. Snakes have long played an important role in voodoo ritual.

sect and to answer devotees' questions about love, luck, money, and the secret thoughts of their masters. In order to divine answers to the questions, the queen acted as a medium, entering a trance in order to "channel" an adder snake that represents the spirit of the serpent god, Damballah. In this process, Damballah takes possession of the medium's body and expresses its desires through her mouth. Moreau de Saint-Mery describes the importance of the snake: "Knowledge of the past, learning of the present, and foreknowledge of the future are all attributed to this snake. The adder is never willing to share its power, or tell its wishes except through the medium of a [houngan or mambo]."[28]

The mambo conducted a slow, sensual dance with the snake, discarding the handkerchiefs that made up her outfit one by one. She laid the snake on the ground and stood over it as the serpent took possession of her. According to Moreau de Saint-Mery, "She shakes, her whole body is convulsed and the oracle speaks through her mouth. Sometimes she flatters and promises happiness, sometimes she utters reproaches. . . . She says whatever she likes, in the name of the adder, to that assembly . . . who never raise the slightest doubt over the most monstrous absurdity. They know nothing else but to obey her or the adder's despotic fiat."[29] In all likelihood these messages were delivered in a hissing voice, with the mambo attempting to imitate the sounds made by a snake.

All devotees received answers to the questions posed earlier, though some were ambiguous. The ceremony continued as the adder was returned to its cage and a goat sacrificed. Its blood was collected in a jar and "used to seal the lips of all present with a vow to suffer death rather than reveal anything and even to inflict [death] on whoever might prove forgetful of such a momentous pledge."[30] This part of the ceremony concluded, the *danse vaudau*, or voodoo dance, began to the sound of furious drumming. The voodoo king drew a black circle with charcoal or gunpowder

"The Delirium Keeps Rising"

In 1797, French scholar M.L.E. Moreau de Saint-Mery wrote *A Civilization That Perished: The Last Years of White Colonial Rule in Haiti*. In the following excerpt, the shocked author describes the activities at a voodoo ceremony where snakes, alcoholic drinks, and sexual trysts add to the pandemonium:

The [voodoo] Queen . . . is the prey to the most violent agitations. From time to time she goes up to the Voodoo snake to seek some new magic and shakes the chest and the little bells with which it is adorned, making them ring out in a very climax of folly. But the delirium keeps rising. It is augmented still more by the use of intoxicating drinks, which in their frenzied state the participants do not spare and which help to sustain them. Faintness and raptures take over some of them and a sort of fury some of the others, but for all there is a nervous trembling which they cannot master. They spin around ceaselessly. And there are some in this species of bacchanal who tear their clothing and even bite their flesh. Others who are only deprived of their senses and have fallen in their tracks are taken, even while dancing, into the darkness of a neighboring room, where a disgusting prostitution exercises a most hideous empire. Finally, weariness brings an end to these afflicting scenes.

on the floor of the room. This was near the *poteau-mitan*, or center pole where the serpent god and spirits purportedly communicate with the people. Nearby an altar was decorated with candles, pictures of Christian saints, and symbols relating to the loa, such as a ritual whistle that symbolizes the hissing of Damballah.

The houngan ordered new recruits to stand in the center of the black circle so that they might be initiated into the sect. The neophytes seemed to be in trances, each one holding a magical charm, according to Moreau de Saint-Mery, "made up of herbs, animal hair, bits of horn, and other things just as disgusting."[31] These neophytes came out of their trance only when the voodoo king hit them on the head with his hand, a wooden spoon, or a cow's neck tendon. They were led to an altar to take an oath of loyalty to the cult. The ceremony continued with the dancers spinning in circles until everyone seemed delirious. Finally, the light of dawn called an end to the festivities as the exhausted voodooists ceased their activity.

Although this ritual took place more than two centuries ago, according to Mêtraux:

> Analyzed in the light of our present knowledge, the words of Moreau de Saint-Mery allow no room for doubt that there existed in Saint-Domingue, towards the end of the eighteenth century, rites and practices which have scarcely changed up to modern times. The authority of the [mambo, her] dress, the importance of the trance, signs drawn on the ground are familiar now as then.[32]

A houngan leads a voodoo ceremony in Togo, West Africa. Houngan (priests) and mambos (priestesses) claim to derive their powers directly from the gods.

Truly Astonishing Knowledge

Today in Haiti and elsewhere where voodoo is practiced, the houngan and mambos continue to act on behalf of the loa. They lead voodoo rituals and ceremonies and interpret

the influence of the loa on the lives of believers. According to Galembo, voodoo clergy also "intercede with the [loa] when a petitioner needs specific help, as with love or work."[33] Houngan and mambos are treated like royalty by devotees who believe that they derive their supernatural insight and power directly from the loa. Their word is as good as the word of the gods, and to defy them would be considered extremely unlucky and possibly deadly.

In addition to possessing purportedly supernatural powers, voodoo clergy must have detailed knowledge of all the spirits, the powers they possess, and the symbols and emblems assigned to them. As Rigaud writes:

> The amount of his knowledge is truly astonishing. The moment his own knowledge fails, he consults the loas in order to increase it. However, it is not only by summoning the loas that he is able to see them. He also often beholds them in dreams or by . . . supernatural . . . sciences such as palmistry, fortune telling by cards, fire, water, or figure-drawings, in which he is often an expert.[34]

It is also required that voodoo kings and queens know the dances, songs, and liturgies, or prescribed rituals and ceremonies, meant to invoke each loa. As Mêtraux writes: "To do so requires perseverance, a good memory, musical aptitude and a long experience of ritual. A good [houngan] is at one and the same time priest, healer, soothsayer, exorcizer, organizer of public entertainments and choirmaster."[35]

"Maladjusted or Neurotic"

With their expertise in voodoo, houngan and mambos act as community leaders who dispense loa-inspired advice to everyone from the poorest farmers to the wealthiest merchants. Acting as de facto psychiatrists, mayors, and celebrities, voodoo clergy are often rewarded handsomely for their

Father to the Community

Voodoo kings, often called "papa" or "father," have a paternal relationship to members of their community, as Maya Deren writes in *Divine Horsemen: Voodoo Gods of Haiti*:

To be a father, he must be wise. He must show, both in the management of his own personal affairs and in the advice which he gives others, that he "knows" about life. And this knowledge covers all provinces of the secular and includes the economic and political spheres. The houngan is expected to know how to do things, many things, all the things, in fact, which a full life experience would have taught a father: how the gate should be repaired; where the bridge should cross the river if it is built; which cow is likely to give good milk; . . . what percentage of real cement should be mixed with the sand so that a wall will not soon crumble; . . . [and] how to write

(for his largely illiterate parish). And he must know these things not only for his own purposes, but because his parish turns to him for such advice and assistance, assuming, as they would of a parent, both the rightness of his knowledge and their right to it.

His political knowledge and prestige are also of enormous importance. For one thing, he cannot hold ceremonies without permission from the police. He must, therefore, be on cordial terms with such officials. It is preferable that he be also on good terms with politically influential persons who will "facilitate" matters. This means that he must know certain sophisticated proprieties and manners: . . . how to receive visitors; how to serve them refreshments; how to conduct himself in town. He must know, in a sense, the ways of a world from which the peasant is distant.

work, garnering wealth as well as respect and awe from the general public.

It is well-known in Haiti, however, that not all houngan and mambos are strictly honest or even sane. Mêtraux writes that many "whom I knew seemed to me to be maladjusted or neurotic. . . . [One] whose name I shall withhold . . . was a rather disturbing person, sickly, perhaps a drug-addict and gifted with a rather odd imagination."[36]

Others are attracted to the power, prestige, and financial gains inherent in the job. Because life in the poverty-stricken nation of Haiti offers so few options for success to people, many become houngan and mambos simply to improve their condition both financially and socially. Some practitioners are more adept than others, however, and it is believed that working with a mediocre houngan or mambo can lead to serious problems such as illness or death, as Rigaud writes:

> The Voodoo mystères require much greater skills and seriousness from the houng'an and the mam'bos than they do from the rest of the people since all Haitians, in accordance with the tradition of the loas, are magically placed under the jurisdiction of the Voodoo priest. The slightest failure on the part of the priests injures not only those subject to this jurisdiction but the mystères themselves.[37]

For this reason, voodoo clergy may be abandoned by the communities they serve if they fail to fulfill their responsibilities in an honest and efficient manner.

Houngan are expected to perform certain rituals to curry the favor of the gods. Here, a houngan decapitates a turkey during a ritual.

The Hounfour

Houngan and mambos work in a hounfour, a voodoo temple where most rites and celebrations take place. These buildings may be on large country estates belonging to a houngan or in simple shacks in a city. Whatever their condition, hounfours contain similar elements including an altar room, small chambers used for various rituals, and a peristyle, or enclosed courtyard where ceremonial dances are held.

Enclosed areas inside the hounfour may be either individual rooms in a single building or a series of small huts. Whatever the layout, one such room, the djévo, is used to examine and initiate new members into the sect. This room is decorated like the inside of a tomb because the initiate symbolically dies and is reborn as a voodooist. Other individual rooms are reserved for worshipping specific loas. All

A voodoo temple decorated with pythons stands in the center of a village in Benin, West Africa. All temples, or hounfours, conform to the same basic design.

are painted with elaborate voodoo designs and symbols, called *vèvès*, that are said to have magical meaning.

The centerpiece of each room is an altar, a square platform about four feet in height, made from a large stone, concrete, or large bricks called cinder blocks. The voodoo altar is called a *pé*, after the Dahomey word *kpé*, meaning "stone." The pé is covered with a decorative cloth and festooned with dozens of special objects used during ceremonies, such as rattles, bells, and whistles. The pé will also hold stones with purported magical powers, flags decorated with symbols of the particular sect, necklaces and bracelets worn during rituals, pictures of Catholic saints, and books that detail voodoo spells and rites.

The doors of altar rooms open out onto the peristyle, which is usually roofed and surrounded by a wall about four feet in height. This allows inquisitive onlookers who are not in the voodoo sect to observe the mass gatherings, healing rites, dances, and rituals that take place in the peristyle. Drums, which are believed to be the voice of the loas, usually hang from the rafters, while long benches are positioned around the perimeter.

The most important item in the peristyle is the poteaumitan, the center post that reaches from floor to ceiling and acts as the center of focus in the voodoo ceremony. The top of this square post, which is another form of the pé, or altar, is said to represent the center of the sky, while the bottom is the center of hell. The post is painted with two interwoven spiral designs that symbolize the snake gods Damballah Wédo, said to represent the architect of the universe, and Aida Wédo, who symbolizes the knowledge of all gods.

While much of Haiti is mired in poverty, violence, and despair, the hounfour is said to be a place of peace within that chaotic nation as avant-garde filmmaker, musician, and author Maya Deren writes in *Divine Horsemen: Voodoo Gods of Haiti*:

The first impression of a hounfor is of grounds well planned and expertly maintained. . . . Immediately inside the formal entrance there are usually two trees sacred to Legba, as patron of gates, entrances and crossroads, and trees sacred to one or another divinity are profusely scattered throughout the grounds. Such trees, since they are sacred, have escaped the fate of being cut down for firewood (a need which has resulted in the critical deforestation of huge parts of Haiti), and they give a hounfor a distinctively cool, shaded and pleasant quality. . . . The grounds are inevitably well-swept and often have flower-beds in informal but colorful arrangement. . . . Almost all the structures are brilliantly whitewashed, unless, in honor of a certain loa, his special hounfor has been painted a pale pink or blue.[38]

Divine Manifestation

The hounfour is the religious and social center for many communities in Haiti, and the temple comes alive during ceremonies that can be held nearly any night of the year. During the rituals, which can last from sunset to sunrise, voodooists enter a trance in which they believe that their soul is temporarily displaced, or possessed, by a specific loa. During this time, the actions and words of the voodooist are said to be those of the loa, not the person possessed. Deren describes the concept: "To understand that the self must leave if the loa is to enter is to understand that one cannot be man and god at once."[39]

When possession occurs, the loa mounts and rides a person as a man rides a horse. Whatever actions that person undertakes in this state are said to be similar to a horse that is expressing the will of its rider, who is known in voodoo as the divine horseman. According to Deren, however, the "horses" rarely remember the event after it is over. She of-

fers this interpretation of the phenomenon: "[The possessed] is not responsible for good or for bad; and he cannot, as a person, himself benefit from that possession. The function and purpose of such divine manifestation is the reassurance and the instruction of the community."[40] The reassurance and instruction are part of the loas proving their dominion over all earthly entities, including people. At the same time, spirit possession makes it possible for humans to interact, however briefly, with the gods.

For many voodooists, the first time this exchange of human soul and godly spirit occurs is during adolescence. Possession may initially occur spontaneously from stress or while attending drum and dance ceremonies at a hounfour. When a youngster does experience the first possession, the particular spirit that rode him or her is identified and discussed with relatives. The residing spirit is then said to be the "master of the head" of the voodooist. A brief initiation

A possessed woman swims in a sacred mud pool in the town of Plaine du Nord, Haiti. Possession allows humans to interact with the gods.

45

ritual is held in which the person's soul is safely stored in a bottle or covered clay pot known as a *pot-de-tète*, interpreted as a receptacle for the head, soul, or mind. The pot-de-tète is stored with dozens of others in a special room at the houn-four. When a person dies, a ceremony is held in which the pot is broken to let the soul escape back into the heavens.

Once someone becomes the horse of a particular spirit, he or she will practice certain rituals or perform specific songs and dances to make the spirit appear. During these ceremonies a string of dozens of spirits may take possession of the voodooist temporarily, but only with permission of the master of the head. Each spirit has its own characteristics, and the possessed will act out roles determined by the spirits. For example, those possessed by the snake god Damballah will slither around on the floor, hissing and flicking the tongue.

The Secret Source of Power

Whatever spirits are on display, they must first be called to the ceremony, which typically begins with drumming. During a normal Haitian voodoo ceremony, the peristyle will fill with as many as two hundred people. The overflow crowds spill out onto the grounds surrounding the temple. Many people work for months on outfits specially designed for the occasion. They may wear large, elaborate homemade masks representing different animals or loas, or they may dress in fantastic costumes reminiscent of Halloween in the United States.

Inside the peristyle food plays an important ceremonial role as a table is filled with delicacies for the loas, including cakes, pastries, custards, chocolate, and pudding, as well as soft drinks, liqueurs, and rum. Sometimes trays holding the cooked meat from a bull, goat, chicken, or pig sacrificed earlier in the day are also on display. After the ceremonies, the foods not eaten on behalf of the loas by the "horses" will be consumed by the houngan, mambos, and their families.

At an appointed hour, a special drumbeat is played that announces the formal beginning of the ceremony as the houngan enters to much fanfare. The crowd performs a short ritualistic dance and falls silent as the houngan loudly launches into a prayer to Damballah Wédo. As the drumming resumes, people sing very loudly over the beats while dancing together in a group. A scene in Port-au-Prince, Haiti, is described by Deren:

Now is the dance which suggests water. Before me the bodies of the dancers undulate with a wave-like motion. . . . The eyes are fixed on the ground, and although the head is steady, the circular movement of the shoulders seems to send it forward, to draw the body after it, over and over; and as the bodies . . . bend towards the earth, the undulation becomes

The meat from the goat this woman is carrying will be placed inside the temple's peristyle as a sacrifice to the loas.

more and more horizontal, until all figures blend into a slow flowing serpentine stream circling the center-post. . . . At such moments one does not move *to* the sound, one *is* the movement of the sound, created and borne by it.[41]

"Their Gods Live in Them"

Houngan and a mambo sing and dance at a voodoo ceremony in Benin. Dancing is a common element in voodoo ceremonies.

The dancing described by Deren is similar at most voodoo rituals, and within thirty minutes, people typically begin to enter into possession trances. Voodooists say these are caused by the loas. However, nonbelievers attribute the trances to the cumulative effects of the rhythmic dance

movements, energetic physical activity, intense heat in the peristyle, and physical exhaustion. Whatever the case, the dancers who are said to be mounted by spirits exhibit bizarre behavior. Some "horses'" bodies jerk violently while others freeze in place. Some fall down as if hit by a club while others dance in a whirling frenzy. Possession is usually not a very pleasant experience and may be accompanied by terror, physical pain, and exhaustion, as Deren writes: "Never have I seen the face of such anguish, ordeal and blind terror as the moment when the loa comes."[42]

After the terror passes, the "horse" takes on the movements of the loa, and observers can immediately recognize the specific spirit present by the dancing movements of the possessed. As dancer and choreographer Katherine Dunham, who was a trained anthropologist, writes in *Dances of Haiti*, "It is the loa that dances, not the individual. . . . Nevertheless, both dance and behavior are according to formula, so much so that an outsider, after frequenting dances, can determine almost as readily as an official which loa has entered."[43]

During this time, the drums and drummers play very important roles in the proceedings, as Lois Wilcken writes in *The Drums of Voodoo*:

> The drummer must know a vast repertoire of drum patterns corresponding to the nations of [loas] and to ritual activities. He must be able to recognize hundreds of Vodou songs and rejoin with the proper rhythm. Most important, he must know how to respond during spirit possession. The drummer is a key agent in spirit possession. The entire collective is careful to prevent the possession of drummers themselves because of the disruption it would create in the ritual flow.[44]

The drumming, dancing, and spirit possession can last until dawn. One by one, the loas purportedly announce that

Drums and Drummers

Drums and drummers play central roles in voodoo ceremonies. In *Spirits of the Night: The Vaudun Gods of Haiti*, Selden Rodman and Carole Cleaver describe the types of drums used at a typical voodoo ritual:

> Drumming in *vaudun* is basic, since its percussions control the bodily movements of participants and its abrupt changes of rhythm and tempo bring on possession. . . . The typical battery of three drums in the [voodoo] ceremony follows Dahomean prototypes. Carved from the trunk of a tree in the shape of a truncated cone, the head—of [bull] or goat-skin—is stretched by means of cords attached to wooden pegs, which may then be hammered to achieve the degree of tautness required by the musician. The largest of the three drums, the *maman* (mother) is struck with the hands or a hooked wooden hammer, either on the taut drumhead or the wooden rim. Its standing drummer controls all rhythms, sometimes on signal from the *houngan* and sometimes on his own. The second drum, *segon*, is played by a musician who holds it between his legs, seated, and beats it with one hand, a forked stick or bow in the other. The smallest third drum, *bula*, is held vertically and struck with two sticks. The second and third drums provide mainly accompaniment. Sometimes a metal bell, an *ogan*, is struck with an iron rod to announce the basic rhythm which the three drums, the *maman* last, will play.

they are satisfied with the ceremony and that it is time to go. As the spirits depart, their "horses" come back to reality, often confused over what transpired. Exhaustion sets in almost immediately, and most return to their normal lives until the next ceremony allows them to channel spirits once again.

Such ceremonies, while native to Haiti, may be repeated throughout the world, from Togo in Africa, to New Orleans and even New York City. While voodooists firmly believe that such possessions are real, scientists and anthropologists have studied Haitian possession-trance phenomena and come to other conclusions. Given the unforgiving circumstances of most Haitians' daily lives, loa possession is said to give a psychological boost to people who cannot find personal satisfaction elsewhere. By masquerading as potent spirits, the people acting as spirit horses seem to experience a taste of a power otherwise unavailable to them. In addition, spirit possession allows them to forget their problems for a night and dance with the divine. As William Sargant writes in *The Mind Possessed*:

> Your god comes to you, possesses you, mounts you, and you become a god yourself. And these very humble people, with very humble lives, are enabled thereby to live lives of comparative happiness because they have found a religion which does bring down their gods to them. And their gods live in them and they live in their gods. . . . To them their gods are real.[45]

Chapter 3

Gods of Voodoo

The voodoo religion revolves around belief in dozens of gods, or loas. Like the Catholic saints that have been incorporated into voodoo, each has its own symbolism, significance, and protective qualities. The voodoo gods are complicated, however. Each one has many meanings, some of them contradictory. Their names, which are often words translated from the African Fon dialect, may be spelled and pronounced several ways depending if the translator is French, Haitian, English, or Spanish.

In Haiti and other places where voodoo is practiced, extraordinary powers are attributed to these complex deities. An unnamed peasant in Marbial, Haiti, explained: "The *loa* love us, protect us and guard us. They tell us what is happening to our relations who live far away, they suggest to us remedies which bring us relief when we are sick. . . . If we are hungry, the *loa* appear to us in a dream and say: 'Take courage: you will earn money' and the promised money comes."[46] Some say loas prevented their drowning, others say the deities killed a rival or brought them a wife. To those who believe, there is nothing that the loas cannot accomplish.

The loas not only intervene supernaturally to prevent disasters but also spread their messages through the mouths of those possessed during voodoo ceremonies. Every voodooist has a specific loa that rides him or her during possession trances, and these spirits are referred to as one's "mother" and "father."

The Rada and Petro

The loas of voodoo are divided into two main families, *Rada* and *Petro*. Rada is named after the town Arada in Dahomey, and the rites associated with these gods are the most elaborate and most consistent with the ancient beliefs of West Africa. The great gods in the Rada pantheon are among the most well-known among voodooists: Legba the gatekeeper, Damballah the serpent, Ogou the god of war, and Gede Nimbo, more often called Papa Ghede, the guardian of the cemetery. These loas, among dozens of other Rada deities, are considered representative of the true spirit of Africa and are honored at the beginning of most voodoo ceremonies. Gerdès Fleurant explains the qualities of these loas, or lwas, in *Vodou*:

Followers of a mambo in Benin kneel around an altar to the god of war as the priestess pours chicken blood over it.

The Rada lwas are *dous* or sweet. These lwas represent . . . the "flower of Guinea" or true spirit of Africa. Their sense of justice is well developed, as they promote the concept of spiritual balance of both the individual and the collective. They are first and foremost the profound and traditional mysteries of Africa, the foundation of the principles by which all in the community live.[47]

In the duality of voodoo, the Petro gods are opposite of the Rada, as black is opposite of white. The name Petro is derived from a hectic voodoo dance, the Dance of Don Pedro, said to have originated in the Congo, possibly named after an eighteenth-century voodoo houngan, Jean-Phillip Pedro. During voodoo rites, dancers of the Don Pedro drank rum mixed with gunpowder, which accelerated their convulsive movements and was said to bring on madness that sometimes resulted in heart failure. Like the bizarre dance that is their namesake, the Petro loas are said to be bitter, not sweet. They symbolize fire and so represent hot tempers, violent behavior, war, bad deeds, and black magic. Those who study voodoo, however, point out that only about 5 percent of voodoo deities are in the Petro family and that tales of black magic, while corresponding to actual events, are extremely rare in voodoo practice.

In the complicated voodoo pantheon, some loas can embrace both Rada and Petro qualities. For example, when Erzulie, the goddess of love, appears in her Rada form, she exhibits a comely manner and speaks in a girlish voice. In her Petro form, Erzulie is lusty and aggressive, speaking in a low growl. In this way she can embody both sides of love, from the romantic to the animalistic.

Endless Variations

Just as the same god can have different, opposing aspects, the deities, or mystère, also symbolize different things to

The Grand Master of the Gods

Voodooists believe that Bondyé, or the Gran Mêt, is the supreme deity who rules over all loas and all people. In *The Faces of the Gods*, Leslie G. Desmangles describes the characteristics attributed to Bondyé:

> Bondye is . . . the king of the universe. He is above all humans and all the loas. He dwells above the heavens; his majesty is unique because it surpasses all. . . . In this omnipotence, Bondye has full hegemony over the universe. His will is absolute. . . . Events in the world occur because he ordains them; without his aid, nothing in the world can happen. Bondye is all-wise, all-knowing. . . . Bondye's wisdom is perfect and infallible. . . . He is said to have more than one thousand eyes which face the four cardinal points of the universe [north, south, east, and west].

He can therefore face all cosmic directions simultaneously. This is why Vodouisants claim that their supreme deity is the discerner of hearts who can see both "the inside and the outside." He sees humankind's hidden secrets—the crafty designs as well as the good intentions. . . .

> Bondye is also the source of all benefits. Through the loas, he is the giver of all good things: children, wealth, good living, good character, and everything else that exists for the good of human beings. Vodouisants believe that even the loas draw their sustenance from Bondye. As the Haitian proverb puts it, "Bondye wills, Bondye takes"—meaning that as the ultimate source of all good things, Bondye exercises his free will in giving or in taking away every good gift.

different people. As novelist, folklorist, and anthropologist Zora Neale Hurston explains in *Tell My Horse*:

> I would not pretend to [know] the name of every mystère in Haiti. *No one* knows the name of every loa because every major section of Haiti has its own local variations. It has gods and goddesses of places and forces that are unknown fifty miles away. The heads of "families" of gods are known all over the country, but there are endless variations of the demigods even in the same localities.[48]

As Hurston writes, the major deities are well-known and each has its own earthly symbols that represent it. These include specific beverages, colors, foods, plants, and days of the week. However, while the loas are considered as individual deities, they are also seen as one overarching aspect of a central supernatural force, the supreme voodoo deity Gran Mèt. Deren describes this concept:

> [Each] major loa . . . contains elements of all the others. Each incorporates, in one way or another, and to varying degrees, life force or fecundity; the protective or paternal; some aspect of both the over- and the under-world or death . . . and some measure . . . of magical immediacy. The loa are distinguished, one from the other, not by their limitations, but by their differing emphases. . . . In a sense, each loa is but an aspect of one central cosmic principle.[49]

In this way, a loa could be compared to a single finger on a hand, working as an individual, in harmony with the others, and also carrying out the will of Gran Mèt who controls them all.

Legba: The Gatekeeper

Voodooists believe that when Gran Mèt made the world, the first loa that he created was the fire of life itself. This fire was manifest in Papa Legba Attibon, the sun. According to religion and anthropology professor Leslie G. Desmangles in the *The Faces of the Gods*: "In Vodou, the sun with which Legba is identified is a regenerative life-force whose rays cause the vegetation to grow and ensure the maturation and sustenance of human life."[50] Without Papa Legba nothing —human, loa, or otherwise—could exist.

It is said that Legba controls access to all other loas. He is the gatekeeper between the earthly world and the cosmos inhabited by the gods. His role is often compared to that of a traffic policeman at a busy intersection. Thus Legba, also known as Master of the Crossroads, facilitates an organized passage of loas, allowing them to take possession of the bodies of the voodooists one by one during rituals. Supplications to Legba implore him to please open the gate between the loas and humans: "Papa Legba, open the gate for me. Attibon Legba, open the gates so we may pass through. Papa; When I will have passed, I thank the loa. . . . Legba who sits on the gate, Give us the right to pass."[51]

Legba not only opens the gate but is also seen as the guardian of gates and fences that safeguard homes. As a protector of roads, he is the god of travel who keeps travelers from harm by evil spirits believed to haunt the highways.

In his important role as the chief loa, Legba's presence is ubiquitous at hounfours. The ritual bonfires in the courtyards are kept perpetually burning to honor him and his picture is painted in the central area, as Desmangles writes:

> Vodou drawings on [peristyle] walls show him as an old man, smoking a pipe; a small sack in which he carries morsels of food dangles by his side from a strap that passes over his shoulder. He totters slowly, leaning on a cane known as a *baton Legba* (Legba's cane). This cane represents a phallus, the source of human life, the symbol of man's virility, and the virtual link between generations.[52]

Unlike most loas, Legba does not have a special ceremonial day of the year. Every day belongs to the gatekeeper, and he must be called before any ceremony begins.

Like all major loas, the Rada Legba has a Petro counterpart, this one known as Mèt Kafou Legba, or "Master Legba of Intersections." Where the Rada deity is seen as the sun and the source of life, the Petro Legba is the moon and a destroyer. In this role, Legba is known as the divine trickster, one who alters important messages and changes fates through accidents, bad luck, or other negative events.

Erzulie: The Goddess of Love

Legba's female counterpart is Erzulie, also known as Ezili-Freda-Dahomey. In her role as the Goddess of Love, Erzulie is seen as the embodiment of feminine beauty, love, and passion. The love song to Erzulie is the most popular in Haiti, after the invocation to Legba.

In her idealized role as the ultimate beautiful, young woman, Erzulie has limitless wealth and access to unearthly luxury. She wears gold jewelry, expensive clothes, and fine French perfume. To please her during ceremonies, a room is set aside and filled with foods and grooming products. All these are the finest quality that her "horse" can afford—the soap is new, the towels are embroidered, the washbasin is shining, the comb is special, and the toothbrush is unused.

A Haitian mambo pours water on her head during a ritual to honor Erzulie, the voodoo Goddess of Love.

Possessed by the Love Goddess

When a voodooist has been taken possession by the Love Goddess Erzulie, or Ezili, an elaborate process takes place, as Alfred Mêtraux explains in *Voodoo in Haiti*:

[The] chosen person is led into [a] room to be dressed and titivated [spruced up]. While this is going on the choir sings the following song:

Ah the lovely woman

Who is Ezili!

Oh, I will give you a present

Before you go away, Abobo [Amen]

At last, in the full glory of her seductiveness, with hair unbound . . . Ezili makes her entrance to the peristyle. She walks slowly, swinging her hips, throwing saucy, ogling looks at the men, or pausing for a kiss or caress. She likes to get presents and give them. . . . She is so fond of men that she instinctively mistrusts women as rivals; she treats them haughtily and greets them by hooking her little finger in theirs. . . . [When] she pretends to speak French, she purposely talks in a high-pitched voice. When she goes back to her boudoir men flock to escort her.

These are laid on a dressing table next to her red and blue dress and jewels. When the "horse" is possessed by Erzulie, he or she bathes, dresses in her clothes, and takes on the role of a seductive love goddess. Since she is said to be a mulatto—half African and half white—the "horse" powders his or her face to lighten the complexion.

Like most voodoo loas, Erzulie is said to have a Catholic counterpart, the Virgin Mary. As Hurston explains, however, this association is inaccurate in many respects.

Erzulie is not the passive queen of heaven and mother of anybody. She is the ideal of the love bed. She is so perfect that all other women are a distortion compared to her. The Virgin Mary and all of the female saints . . . have been elevated, celebrated for their abstinence. Erzulie is worshipped for her perfection in giving herself to mortal man. To be chosen by a goddess is an exaltation for men to live for.[53]

While she is adored by men, like other loas, Erzulie has a Petro side that includes rivalry, jealousy, vengeance, and discord. When a man has bad luck, it might be said that the Goddess of Love is punishing him for ignoring her. If he is in love with a mortal woman, the unlucky man has to choose between Erzulie and his wife or girlfriend. This may result in misfortune, ill health, and even death. If the man chooses to please Erzulie, he must put aside a bedroom in his house dedicated to her. His spouse may not enter except to keep the room spotless and the bed perfectly made. Oftentimes divorce is the end result. For this reason women hate and fear Erzulie, their spiritual rival. Despite the dangers, there are men who join the cult of Erzulie, renouncing earthly women for the goddess.

Damballah the Good Serpent of the Sky

Erzulie represents the most influential and feared of the female loas. One of the most powerful male spirits is Damballah Wédo, the ancient father who helped Gran Mèt create the universe. Also known as the Good Serpent of the Sky, Damballah is represented as a snake traveling the arch that the sun makes across the heavens. Sometimes he travels this curved path with his female counterpart, Aida, the rainbow. Together these two loas represent the union of a man and a woman, the source of life on earth.

Damballah is the head of the Rada family and is said to live in the heavenly tree of spiritual wisdom. Although the great snake possesses all of the knowledge of the universe, it is impossible to receive it from him since he only communicates in a barely intelligible hissing. As Desmangles explains, "In his cosmic grandeur and venerable wisdom he refuses to be bothered with the pretty precision of human speech."[54] Despite this trait, Damballah is adored because of his paternal love.

Damballah is said to be responsible for the life-giving rains that sustain humankind. He is symbolized by things that represent the beauty in nature, and his food offerings include fruit such as melons, pineapples, bananas, oranges, and apples. Fine desserts, sweet liqueurs, and the showiest flowers are also gathered to honor him. Those who regularly make offerings to Damballah expect good luck, as one un-named houngan stated: "It is possible for you to have a grand situation and it is even possible to become a minister or pres-ident if you serve Papa Damballah faithfully. But yes!"[55]

After opening voodoo ceremonies with the song to Legba, houngan invoke Damballah with the words: "O Wedo, calling Wedo, O Wedo there, it is Damballah Wedo."[56] After prayers, drummers play a sacred rattle—a hollow gourd covered with a mesh of snake vertebrae—that makes a hiss-ing sound associated with the serpent. The drums join in to play the rhythms for Damballah's ceremonial snake dance, the *yanvalou*. Dancers mimic the motions of serpents, wrig-gling their entire bodies and sometimes falling on the ground to slither like snakes.

Ghede, Loa of the Dead

While Damballah, as the life force of the universe, does not have a negative side, he stands in opposition to Ghede (or Gede), who rules death, destruction, and the end of time. Seen as the opposite of the sun, Ghede is the dark abyss where the sun is extinguished when it drops into the sea each night. Ghede dresses in black and lingers at the cross-roads of death where all people must eventually travel. In this role, he represents neither good nor evil, love nor de-spair, but the inevitable end of life. He is the keeper of the cemetery but also the guardian of history and the past.

The symbols of Ghede are those of death: skulls, bones, the black wooden cross, the pickax and shovel of the grave digger, and piles of stones representing gravestones. Rooms set aside for him in hounfours are decorated in the ghoulish appearance of a graveyard. These rooms contain sacrificial

A mambo in Port-au-Prince, Haiti, lifts a bottle of strongly peppered rum over her head in honor of Ghede, the loa of death.

offerings including a strong rum spiked with twenty-one of the hottest spices available—a drink so peppery only Ghede himself can swallow it.

Ghede is often consulted concerning all manner of life-changing events, including marriages, birth, and major undertakings. Believers say that the future can only be blessed if the past, the realm of Ghede, is satisfied. During ceremonies, they sing the song of the cemetery, according to Deren "a jerky, blood-chilling, hypnotic melody. No one who has . . . heard that hysterical 'ke ke ke ke ke' of the grave-digger, could ever forget it."[57] Ghede's speaking voice is equally disturbing, a high, nasal sound that voodooists say is the sound a corpse would make if it could talk.

Ghede uses his voice to convey shocking, but false, sexual stories about community members. He taunts listeners and embarrasses them with the foulest language while he gestures obscenely. This breaking of taboos—common in death mythology of many ancient cultures—is said to represent the sinner in all people. The sexual theme is seen in pictures of Ghede painted on hounfour walls, as Desmangles explains:

> Pictures of him . . . show a man with enlarged nostrils indicating breathing, a symbol of life, but with petrified arms and feet. His large [body] is depicted as that of a skeleton, a symbol of death. In contrast his erect phallus is large . . . for [voodooists] say that when he walks, the movements of his body recall the sexual act.[58]

The Uninvited Loa

Like death, Ghede often appears uninvited and unwanted. Taking possession of an unwilling "horse" during ceremonies, Ghede exhibits an insatiable appetite and will piggishly eat all the ceremonial foods laid out for other loas. Because death consumes life, Ghede's hunger cannot be stanched and he uses both hands to stuff food into his mouth. When the food is gone, he often shrieks, cries, screams, creates an uproar, and demands more while falsely blaming voodooists for stealing the food he consumed or carried out of the hounfour and buried. This disruption can bring a quick end to ceremonies, and those in the midst of spirit possession can find that the loas have suddenly abandoned them without warning.

In his Petro manifestation, Ghede is even more of a negative force. His hunger is so ravenous that he begins to consume himself, biting into his own arms. Onlookers must save him from himself and pry his teeth from his own flesh.

Not all voodooists dislike being possessed by Ghede. Those in his cult, whether male or female, dress in tall top hats, striped pants, and black tailcoats, an outfit traditionally worn by government officials attending funerals. They wear sunglasses with dark lenses because Ghede spends so much time underground his eyes are sensitive to light. If people possessed by Ghede do not have the sunglasses, they will steal them off the faces of bystanders. Sometimes a "horse" ridden by Ghede becomes so obsessed with sunglasses that he or she will wear four or five pairs on the face and head. To simulate his ghostly complexion, Ghede "horses" put layers of talcum powder on their faces. They also stuff cotton in their nostrils and ears and wind linen bandages around their chins, imitating the traditionally prepared corpse in Haiti.

A Haitian man with talcum powder on his face and sunglasses balances a human skull on his head in tribute to Ghede.

In the 1920s devotees of Ghede marched into the office of President Louis Borno and extorted money from him.

Ghede is said to have a wife, Madame Brigitte, who also rules cemeteries. Brigitte had a child with Ghede named General Jean-Baptiste the Outliner. His inexplicable job is to draw chalk outlines around the edges of graves. Ghede's helpers include General Dig, who digs graves, Ramasseur-de-Croix, Collector of the Crosses, and Baron Samedi, the keeper of the grave-digging tools who is also known as Three-Spades, Three-Picks, and Three-Hoes.

While there are many negative influences associated with Ghede, his devotees often have unchallenged power. In the 1920s, a group of houngan dressed as Ghede walked past armed guards into Haiti's National Palace, singing the loa's eerie song. The Ghedes danced into President Louis Borro's office and demanded money. The president, a believer in voodoo, gave the Gods of Death what they asked for, as Deren writes: "Ghede had made his point. Death, who has consumed so many heroes, bows before no man and will remind even the most illustrious that one day he too will be consumed."[59] The Ghedes took the president's money and gorged themselves on food. A song was written about the event that remains one of the most popular in Haiti.

Walk Among the Immortals

There are hundreds of other gods and goddesses in the voodoo pantheon, each with their own interesting mythology relating to earth and the supernatural. For example, when Sogbo the loa of lightning and Bade the god of wind act together, they wake up Agau, the violent deity of rainstorms. "Horses" ridden by Agau imitate the sounds of thunder and may become so violently possessed that they die.

What the Gods Can Do

Each voodoo loa, or mystère, has its own powers and its own reasons for choosing to appear during ceremonies. According to Milo Rigaud in *Secrets of Voodoo*, a mystère can mount a person for the following reasons:

To protect him.

To confer upon him a power or a faculty that he needs for the successful accomplishment of a task, and which he does not ordinarily have. To permit him, for example, to swim to land in case of a shipwreck, if he does not know how to swim. . . .

To permit him to remove himself with supernatural speed.

To cure him of illness or to prevent him from suffering.

To give him counsel. In this case, those who speak to the possessed person repeat to him the advice that the loa gave during the [possession].

To give some other person a treatment, or simply to prescribe or compose a remedy.

To punish the "horse" for some offense. In this case . . . the mystère may refuse to leave—to dismount the "horse"—for hours or days, determined to exhaust him as much as possible. . . .

To point out some [unknown] ritual.

To give warning of danger threatening an individual or the community.

To preside over, or to assist at a ritual ceremony.

To come and get a sacrificial offering.

Many loas are truly bizarre. The "Bull with Three Testicles" creates within his devotees destructive rage that can only be stopped when they are fed a handful of grass. The loa Pin'ga eats razor blades. Other loas drink rum through their noses, ears, and even eyes. No matter how strange their behavior or how evil their deeds, each loa has cadres of devotees who base their lives on the perceived whims of the gods. In a region of grinding poverty, where daily survival often depends on long hours of manual labor, the loas provide believers with wealth, power, and adventure. Whether they are real or figments of the imagination is perhaps beside the point. To be possessed by loas is to be part of a celestial force that allows devotees to walk among the immortals in the cosmic world—and be removed from the harsh reality of daily life.

Chapter 4

Healing and Positive Powers

Houngan and mambos, or voodoo priests and priestesses, take on many roles. They are community leaders, spiritual guides for voodoo devotees, and directors of ceremonies where hundreds of people are possessed by loas. Much of the prestige afforded houngan and mambos, however, comes from their role as healers. For this reason, healing activities are said to account for more than half of all voodoo activity. Voodoo doctors heal with herbs, faith healing, with the help of loas, and even with modern medicine.

In Haiti, with only one medical doctor per twelve thousand people, houngan and mambos treat everything from headaches to cancer. Unlike medical doctors who use scientific methods to treat the physical causes of illness, voodoo practitioners believe that many diseases are caused by angry loas or evil spells put to work by an enemy. This guiding principle leads voodooists to treat the purported "supernatural" causes of an ailment, rather than the physical. To do so, the healers go into a possession trance through intensive drumming, dancing, and singing in order to channel the loas. The deities purportedly reveal cures that might include drinking herbal teas, carrying magic charms, or making offerings to specific loa. If the patient is bothered by an evil spirit, the voodoo doctor might channel a Petro loa that rules the world of negative energy and black magic, seeking a cure through sacrificial offerings or other methods.

A few houngan and mambos provide their services free of charge and accept donations from grateful patients that might include livestock, foods, clothing, or other valuables. Most voodoo practitioners charge for their services, and some may be as expensive as a medical doctor. If payment is not forthcoming, the healers threaten to enlist the loas to make the patient sick again. If the money is still not delivered, the voodoo doctor may announce the intent to ask the loa to kill the patient. This rarely happens, however. Most patients understand the financial arrangement when they consult a voodoo healer and understand that payment must be made. In return, they demand that they get their money's worth and that the doctor's cure must work properly. Word spreads quickly about houngan and mambos who fail to cure their patients, and they are soon without customers.

Healing the Body and Soul

With the expense of paying a houngan or medical doctor, most sick Haitians first treat themselves with herbal and folk medicine. For example, a peasant might drink herbal tea to treat headaches, colds, laryngitis, and other minor ailments. If this fails to cure the patient, he or she will consult with a voodoo doctor who will try to determine if the ailment is physical or supernatural. One method for doing so is described by Haskins: "A conjure-doctor summoned to attend a case of mysterious illness in a family will frequently begin his examination by putting a small piece of silver into the mouth or hand of the sufferer. Should the silver turn black, there is no doubt [the client is under an evil spell]."[60] In such a case, the conjurer can take several steps. The first is to search the patient's home for an object that could be

Before seeking the services of a houngan or medical doctor, most sick Haitians like these men try first to treat themselves with herbal and folk remedies.

responsible for the pain. For example, if a patient suffers from headaches, an enemy might have placed an evil spell on a stone and put it under the victim's pillow, hidden it under a bed, or put it around the hats in a closet.

If the pain continues, or if no obvious causes are found, a ceremony will be conducted on the patient's behalf. In this case, the healer must enter the invisible spiritual world where the illness purportedly originated. The doctor must then remove the negative energy from the patient.

An illness attributable to supernatural causes is said to affect the patient's emotional, mental, and physical cores. The negative spirits first affect a person's emotional well-being by making him or her feel depressed or anxious. When the supernatural sickness enters the mental region, the mind makes the patient conscious of the ailment or of some event that might have resulted in a voodoo curse being placed on him or her. Finally, after harming the emotional and attached itself to the heart of the seated one. All around the [room] there were lights, like tiny blue-and-gold stars, sparkling, exploding, then fading and dying, as new lights took their place.[62]

Moments later, the event was over and there was Yabofe sitting alone. The houngan stood, fell on his knees before the patient, and hugged him tightly. Heaven claims to have then seen a blue light emanate from the houngan and surround both men. After a few minutes, Yabofe backed away toward the corner of the room, where there were two chickens. Picking them up by their feet the houngan swung them violently at the patient, hitting him repeatedly from head to toe. This done, Yabofe ripped the heads off the chickens, threw their bodies to the floor, and returned to his chair with his eyes closed and his chin on his chest. Heaven describes the end of the healing ceremony: "Then this old man, this cripple who had been carried by his family to meet Yabofe, stood up and walked away unaided. . . . Yabofe looked up weakly and smiled."[63]

Just how this was possible is a matter of debate. A believer would say that a specific loa took possession of Yabofe and healed the patient with cosmic energy. The ghostly image

Haitian voodoo devotees offer white candles in prayer during a ritual. Each candle color has a different meaning.

reported by Heaven was the loa using the houngan's astral body, defined as another body connected by a cord to every human. The astral body is said to travel throughout the world by itself as the "real" body stays behind. This scenario is implausible to many. For example, philosophy professor and author of the *Skeptic's Dictionary* Robert Todd Carroll writes on the Astral Projection Web site: "There is scant evidence to support the claim that anyone can project their mind, soul, psyche, spirit, astral body, etheric body, or any other entity to somewhere else on this or any other planet."[64]

Magical Powders and Charms

Another controversial form of positive conjuring, or the summoning of spirits, relies on voodoo magic, as distinguished from the voodoo religion as practiced in Haiti, Africa, and elsewhere. Voodoo magic makes use of spells, charms, and talismans believed to offer supernatural powers or protection. Those practicing magic also use symbolic ritual behavior, such as chanting a prayer while lighting candles. Spells are cast using charms, rituals, and prayers in

Haitian women petition a god for health and prosperity before a candlelit altar decorated with religious symbols.

Making a Magical Charm

In 1929 William A. Seabrook traveled to Haiti where a mambo, a houngan, and a sorcerer, or *bocor*, made a magical charm, called a *ouanga*. Seabrook described the ceremony in *The Magic Island*:

[A] square red cloth, like a napkin . . . was to be the covering of my *ouanga* packet. Bright ribbons, red and yellow, lay beside it, and also feathers brilliantly dyed. In little, separated piles . . . were balsam leaves, leaves of the castor-bean plant, roots of the lime tree; a saucer of flour, a saucer of ashes, a bottle of *clairin* [white rum], a bottle of perfume, a tiny iron crucifix.

[While mambo Maman Célie and houngan Papa Théodore chanted to Papa Legba] old Théodore took some of the roots and leaves, mixed them in a brazier, charred them over a fire . . . then pounded them together in a mortar. . . . A *bocor* (magician) filled his mouth with *clairin* and sprayed it, sputtering, over all the paraphernalia . . . to drive away evil spirits. . . . [The] *bocor* began picking up balsam leaves and castor-bean leaves, one by one, marking each with a chalked cross and depositing it on the napkin, until a new pile was made there. Atop these leaves he now laid the crucifix, also a tuft of hair (tied together with thread) which had been cut previously from the central crown of my head; a paring from my right thumb-nail, and a small square cut from a shirt which had been worn next to my skin. . . . The *bocor*, with a small glowing brand from the fire, touched off successively three little piles of gunpowder . . . to drive away evil spirits . . . [and I made a wish before the sack was tied up].

order to influence the loas to grant wishes concerning wealth, health, luck, and love.

These spells can also be used to try to achieve nefarious ends through so-called black magic. Since, however, voodooists believe that any evil spells they cast will eventually be turned back on them, most claim to practice only white, or positive, magic. In Haiti, those wishing to utilize this form of magic consult with professional houngan and mambos known as *boko, bocor*, or "sorcerers." These conjurers are said to "work with both hands"[65] as one hand makes magic while the other serves the loas. Whether used for positive or negative ends, voodoo magic is sometimes called hoodoo to distinguish it from the voodoo religion as practiced in Haiti, Africa, and elsewhere.

In New Orleans, a man and a woman pose in front of a hoodoo diagram they have drawn in the street. Hoodoo originated from West African folk magic practices.

According to the Common Misconceptions About Vodoun Web site:

> Hoodoo . . . [which] also has its origins in West Africa . . . is the "folk magic" of the common people in West Africa. . . . From so-called "love potions," to taking vengeance upon an enemy, Hoodoo is largely what has survived the religious persecution of the Africans enslaved in the New World. . . . Hoodoo blended with acceptable Native American & European folklore and practice, but the actual methods and power behind it remained completely African.[66]

Luck Stones and Snake Bones

A typical magic spell was described by William A. Seabrook in his 1929 book *The Magic Island*. Seabrook writes of a female boko named Maman Célie who created a magic love powder at the request of her grandson Paul, who had been rejected by a beautiful young woman named Ti-Marie. Maman Célie instructed Paul to trap a hummingbird, which was then killed and dried in the sun. After the bird was sufficiently brittle, the boko ground it into powder with a wooden pestle and mortar while chanting: "Wood of the woods, bird of the woods, woman you were created by God. Bird of the woods, fly into her heart. I command you in the name of three Marys and in [the rainbow loa] Ayida's name."[67] After other esoteric and mumbled words, the boko mixed the hummingbird powder with a few drops of Paul's blood and the pollen of flowers that grow in the jungle. This mixture was transferred into a goatskin pouch and given to the young man.

The following Saturday evening, at a local dance, Paul threw the hummingbird dust into the face of Ti-Marie. The results were described by Seabrook: "[Half] blinded, with the dust in her eyes and nostrils and mouth, she spat like a young wildcat, and cried out that she would kill him—but she lay with him that night in the forest, and on Monday morning he fetched her home."[68]

Seabrook doubts that the young lady would have gone to Paul without the magic charm, known as an *ouanga*. A skeptic might point out, however, that after the young man showed his intentions, Ti-Marie may have decided to give him a chance. In any event, ouanga like the one made by Maman Célie are commonly used for protection, luck in gambling, health of a newborn, shelter from storms, and almost every other aspect of life left to fate. And the contents of an ouanga can be quite complex. Seabrook writes of one charm carried by a soldier who wished to survive battle. This ouanga contained "luck stones, snake bones, lizard jaws, squirrel teeth, bat bones, frog bones, black hen feathers and bones, black lamb wool, dove hearts, mole skins, images of wax and clay, candy made from brown sugar mixed with liver, mud, [sulfur], salt, alum, and vegetable poisons."[69]

There is little doubt that all the ingredients were selected for symbolic reasons and meant to impart magical qualities. The animal parts are likely tied to various loas, either as representative animals or as items used in sacrifice to the spirits. Mud may have been made from dirt gathered from a crossroads, domain of the great loa Legba, while wax and clay effigies represent various loas or magical symbols. Other things commonly found in ouanga include personal items such as fingernails, hair, or sweat-soaked cloth taken from the person wearing the charm or meant to be affected by it.

A Haitian woman tastes a potion. Magic potions are concocted to provide protection and luck.

The Gris-Gris Bag

In New Orleans, charms similar to Haitian ouanga are known as gris-gris (pronounced "gree-gree") bags, mojo bags, or medicine bags. These small, red flannel or chamois bags are worn either pinned to the shirt near the heart, around the neck, or even in the underwear. Like the ouanga, they contain items such as stones, bones, feathers, money, hair, and fingernails. Although there is no scientific explanation for the alleged powers of the gris-gris bag, New Orleans practitioner Ray T. Marlbrough offers his rationalization:

> The gris-gris bag, as with any other talisman or amulet, acts as a [mental and] spiritual support; it implies faith. It serves to intensify the faith in yourself that through the help of the gris-gris bag you will obtain this or receive that. . . . Faith alone is not enough. One must be patient. Patient, because not all desires will materialize quickly. . . . But if you hold onto your faith and remain patient, the gris-gris bag can serve as a key to open the door to . . . future happiness.[70]

Shops in New Orleans and elsewhere offer all manner of oils, candles, incense, powders, herbs, spell books, and other paraphernalia used to make gris-gris bags. This "do-it-yourself" magic is voodoo at its most basic and accessible. People buy lavender to bring love, cloves for passion, nutmeg for money, cinnamon for success, mustard seed for luck, thyme for health, and bay leaves to break, or "uncross," an evil spell. These are combined with lucky stones such as amethyst, garnet, topaz, and turquoise.

Such talismans are often used in conjunction with other voodoo magic. Voodooists in New Orleans, Haiti, and elsewhere who want to boost the power of their charms may anoint their bodies with oil consecrated with purportedly magical herbs. For example, a suspect hoping to face a

The Gris-Gris Bag

In New Orleans, voodooists who want good luck, money, or love wear a gris-gris bag. The ingredients and powers of the gris-gris are explained in "the Voodoo Queen" on the Parascope Web site:

Gris-gris (pronounced "gree-gree") comes from the French word *gris* which means gray, hence a combination of black (negative) and white (positive) magic. In New Orleans, positive charms were called "juju," and negative were called "mojo"—terms which emanated from African tribal beliefs. Gris-gris was the most powerful of all charms and also the most expensive, and it could be used for good or ill.

Gris-gris was a potion of herbs and natural or decaying matter, from the mundane to the bizarre, sometimes including powdered brick, ochre, cayenne pepper, fingernail clippings, human hair, and animal skin (usually reptil-ian)—all tossed into a small leather bag. Thankfully, this mixture was not ingested, but was worn around the neck from a string, or left near the intended object of the charm. It supposedly brought either good or bad luck, depending on what you believed in. The real power of the gris-gris lay in the psychology of the object of the charm. The power of suggestion, more than anything else, was the real power behind the gris-gris. It was essentially a non-ingested, magical placebo.

Gris-gris lives on today in popular culture. Even nowadays in the New Orleans area, it is not uncommon to hear the expression "to put gris-gris on it," meaning to perform some task so astonishingly well it seems as if magic is being used. Or the expression can be used with a negative meaning, as if a hex were placed on a particular action.

friendly judge in court might rub his body with a concoction made from olive oil, carnation petals, anise seed, cinnamon, and the root of a ginger-like plant called galangal. Someone hoping to find a mate could wear an oil infused with loveage herb, grated lemon peel, and lemon flowers.

A believer might also use a lucky wash, described by Marlbrough as "an herb mixture usually steeped in water and used to sprinkle on or wash down the floor of a home, business, mailbox, etc. It is designed to attract or dispel certain influences. . . . [For example, if] your business has walk-in customers, wash down the entrance floor, the door handle, and the aisle."[71] Believers also sprinkle voodoo washes around the grounds of a home to repel thieves, around a card table to bring gambling luck, or inside a home to promote peace and tranquility.

Suggestively named premade washes, oils, and incense are available in voodoo shops. For example, someone hoping to win the lottery might buy Winning Number Incense at the local voodoo shop. Grandma's Lucky Hand Oil would be used to help a gambler win at dice or cards. Believers can also buy Stop Evil Floor Wash, Jinx Killer Oil, Make Your Wish Oil, Strong Love Cologne, and even Money Soap.

Skeptics point out that voodoo oils, incense, soaps, and washes are most often sold for great profit to vulnerable people down on their luck. Yet regardless of whether these products work as advertised, they appear to serve some basic need. Haskins writes, "People have been comforted by knowing that they retained an element of control over any threatening force. There's no charm that can't be broken;

A typical voodoo shop in New Orleans offers something for every believer, from jinx removal to wish fulfillment.

Caption here. Caption here. Caption here.

one needs only to find a practitioner who has a sufficiently powerful prescription to break it."[72]

Folk Spells

Other methods for casting spells do not rely on powders, oils, incense, and washes. These require devotees to make their own charms. The ingredients in these folk spells have been passed down from one generation to the next for hundreds of years. Some are very simple. For example, a person wishing for good luck in court is instructed to write the names of the twelve apostles in two columns on a piece of paper, rip it in half, and put one piece in each shoe.

Love spells are perhaps the most common in voodoo, and there are many examples of ways to attract it, keep it, and even repel it. To attract a man, a woman is instructed to blend rose petals, orange flowers, and honey in water. She should then write the man's name and her name on nine lumps of sugar and dissolve them in the water. This done,

A voodoo altar in a New Orleans home contains many religious symbols, including the Virgin Mary. Offerings of money have been placed all about the altar.

the woman is told to burn a pink candle in this mixture for nine days. Other love potions are decidedly more disgusting, as Haskins gives an altogether different recipe: "Bathe your feet to soften the dry skin thereon. Scrape off some of the dry skin and heat it until it is dry enough to be powdered. Put it in any beverage and give it to the person to drink. The person will follow you all the time."[73]

Some of these spells can be quite macabre. In Haiti, for example, good luck charms are often made from bones, and one spell instructs the voodooist to dig up a corpse and take the little finger bone from the left hand. This is to be soaked in alcohol for nine days, taken back to the graveyard, and reburied. For the next nine days the conjurer pours sweet milk over the grave that was disturbed. On the tenth day the finger is dug up, put in a red flannel bag, and carried at all times. Those who do not wish to go to such extremes may dig in the forest for ginseng or other roots that are in the shape of a human hand.

Millions of people the world over believe in the magical abilities of voodoo spells and charms. While this magic remains controversial and unproved, perhaps it is no different from people buying lottery tickets when the odds of winning are 55 million to 1. It is often simple human nature to believe that there are magical answers to life's problems. Believers point out that people do win the lottery against the odds, and that some may win the love of a person who once ignored them. As long as people are unhappy, they will try to change the forces of nature by petitioning the deities and using occult practices such as voodoo spells to deliver to them their heart's desire.

Chapter 5

Black Magic and Zombies

Millions of people the world over believe in voodoo, attend voodoo ceremonies, and practice its rituals. These people believe that the loas, or deities, take possession of their bodies and ride them like horses. This process imparts cosmic knowledge and puts believers in touch with the gods. Many of these devotees also believe in voodoo magic and practice it in order to improve their luck and bring love and success into their lives. Voodoo also has a dark side, however, and has long been associated with black magic and zombies of the living dead. While these negative forces have often been sensationalized in books, magazines, and movies, few would deny the existence of eerie coincidences that seem to have no other explanation. As Mêtraux points out: "The scenes of black magic . . . the mysterious deaths and the whole disquieting world of the *boko* [sorcerers] . . . and *zombi* . . . are taken from perfectly straightforward accounts which may be heard . . . in the country and in the popular quarters of Port-au-Prince."[74]

Some voodoo practitioners are embarrassed by this aspect of their religion. They consider the lurid tales to be folklore—that is, unfounded myths passed down from one generation to the next. Others say, however, that voodoo has been used to sicken and kill enemies, drive rivals insane, and even place snakes and spiders inside a victim's body. Just how many people try this—and how effectively—is a matter of debate, as Haskins writes:

> It is extremely difficult nowadays to find a practitioner who will admit engaging in malign conjure. . . . Frank Hendricks [who sells voodoo charms, candles, and oils] in New Orleans, estimates that only about two percent of the [voodoo practitioners] with whom

A voodoo priestess lights candles at a New Orleans shrine. Some practitioners engage in black magic.

he has come in contact . . . have practiced un-abashedly evil conjure.[75]

Hendricks does acknowledge, however, that a larger percentage practice a milder form of black magic. These people cast spells hoping to force annoying neighbors to move or to create troubles for difficult bosses, ex-lovers, or other adversaries.

While there may be few who will say publicly that they work with black magic, most voodoo devotees believe in its power. In Haiti, for example, most people do not attribute sickness to germs or infection. Rather, most believe that illness and bad luck are caused by dark forces such as unhappy loas or evil sorcerers. As Mêtraux writes, "Unfortunately rural society has plenty of neurotics or simply troubled and downcast [people] who are quick to suggest that an illness is not 'from God,' that an accident is surrounded with suspicious circumstances and that a death was not due to natural causes."[76]

Sending of the Dead

Whether black magic is superstition or reality, the climate of fear is very real for believers. In Haiti, members of the secret society the *Culte des Morts*, or Cult of the Dead, are allegedly grave robbers who mutilate corpses and use the pieces to cast evil spells. While few outsiders have ever witnessed their rituals, it is said that the cultists gather for ceremonies at altars piled high with human skulls and bones. They dress like Ghede, the loa of the graveyard, and drag pickaxes, shovels, and black crosses to rural cemeteries late at night. After conducting various ceremonies, they rob fresh graves of their bodies and take them back to their hounfour. Seabrook describes how the corpse is used by the Cult of the Dead:

The necromantic uses which they make of various parts of the corpse are thoroughly authenticated in many verifiable cases. . . . They rub grease made from the brains upon the edges of machetes and tools, so that they will be intelligent and cut more accurately; on the head of the hammer so that it will know always where to strike; upon the sights of a gun so that the bullet will reach its mark. The heart they dry and use to give courage to weak persons who eat small portions of it or carry bits of it in a tiny bag strung around their necks. From other parts of the body are concocted ouangas . . . charms for various purposes, benevolent and malevolent. The skull and bones become a part of the permanent altar paraphernalia.[77]

One of the most malevolent deeds committed by the Cult of the Dead and other evil boko is the Sending of the Dead. Casting this spell purportedly causes several spirits of dead people to embed themselves in the body of a victim, who is expected to spit up blood, to be unable to eat, and to die within days.

To activate such a spell, the malevolent conjurer must appear at a graveyard at midnight with an offering of chopped bananas and sweet potatoes. These are laid in front of a black cross representing Ghede. The conjurer then picks up one handful of grave dirt for each dead spirit he wishes to employ. This dirt is spread on a path often trod by the victim. When the unfortunate individual steps on or over the dirt, the deadly spirits will enter his or her body.

Passing the Chicken

Those who wish to use the dead to harass, but not kill, the living employ a different method of Sending of the Dead. When someone dies in the victim's home, a boko will secretly pound two nails into a roof beam in the room where the death occurred. These nails are said to hold the soul of the dead, against its will, in the room. The unhappy soul then takes revenge upon the victim who inhabits the house.

Modern Medicine and a Voodoo Cure

Researchers have tried to find out how voodoo doctors can cure patients who are haunted by the dead, and have come up with some interesting theories. In 1992, an American doctor, C.K. Meador, described a case in the *Southern Medical Journal*, where a man claimed that after an argument with a voodoo conjurer, the boko had sent the spirits of dead people to kill him. The victim stopped eating and was hospitalized. Although he was being fed intravenously, he was dazed and near death. In *What Are the Chances?* medical researcher Bart Holland explains how a doctor used his knowledge of voodoo to cure the man:

> In front of the patient's terrified wife and relatives, the doctor in charge of the case "revealed" to the patient that he himself had recently had a violent argument with the voodoo priest about the patient, and that under dire physical threats from the doctor the voodoo practitioner had divulged the nature of the patient's problem. Thanks to voodoo, a lizard inside the patient was consuming all his food and his guts as well. After this explanation, the doctor then administered an emetic injection [to cause vomiting], and through sleight of hand produced a lizard at the end of the vomiting. The patient fell asleep, woke the next morning with a ravenous appetite, and was discharged in a week.

Mêtraux writes of a woman named Atenaize who claims to have been cursed this way:

> Atenaize, who had complained a great deal about the persecutions she had suffered from her dead husband, had discovered two suspicious nails in a beam of her hut and had had them removed. Unfortunately in the process one of them fell to the ground and was never found. She attributes all her troubles to this lost nail.[78]

Such curses have been said to make victims physically ill, drive them mad, or even cause suicide. Scientific research addressing these phenomena is sparse, and reports of controlled tests of different theories are nonexistent. However, some believe that the victims are so convinced of the reality of black magic that they simply die of fear. In *What Are the*

Chances? medical researcher Bart Holland offers a theory as to how voodoo spells can sicken or kill their victims:

> [Such] illnesses . . . have a physical cause. They are the result of the physical effects of tremendous mental stress. . . . [It] is obvious that extreme fear can cause a fatal heart attack. . . . Clearly not coincidental, the deaths following voodoo spells are caused by some form of exaggerated, negative placebo effect rather than by the direct mechanisms claimed by the voodoo practitioners. The evidence for the power of suggestion as the origin of physical problems among the "hexed" is strong: voodoo death only occurs if the victim and all his or her friends and relatives believe in the power of the voodoo priest to cause it. They must all believe that the particular spell will be fatal and treat the victim as they would treat any individual facing imminent death, in order for the illusion to be complete and effective. Nonetheless, there's a physical explanation here.[79]

Perhaps it is the power of suggestion that allows some houngan and mambos to effectively treat spells such as the Sending of the Dead. The patient is laid out like a corpse at a funeral, and prayers, offerings, and invocations to the loas are made. The voodoo doctor approaches and violently throws magical water in the patient's face. The healer then grabs a hen and repeatedly passes it over the victim's body. This cure, called *pase poul*, literally "pass the chicken," is used to transfer the dead spirits to the chicken. When the ritual is complete, the bird is grasped by the neck and whirled around until its head twists off. The ceremony complete, the evil is purportedly banished. If Holland's theories are correct, such elaborate and violent rituals could ease the extreme mental stress of those who believe they are under an evil spell, whereupon physical healing can begin.

Killing and Crossing

While professional conjurers are said to be able to create misery by the Sending of the Dead, people can use less elaborate ways to try to cause harm. Folk spells similar to those used in white magic are also used in the service of evil. Just as writing someone's name on a lump of sugar is said to bring love, writing a name on a piece of paper and burying it in a miniature coffin with a dead black cat and a dead chicken purportedly will cause the person named to die.

A malevolent conjurer who wishes to torment an adversary rather than kill him might cast a spell to create a long, lingering illness. To watch an enemy suffer and waste away is said to provide greater satisfaction to the boko. Many of the spells aimed at this evil task involve leaving a cursed potion at the victim's home. For example, an old folk recipe calls for the conjurer to boil bark and roots from a persimmon tree and fig tree and mix the liquid with dust taken from the graveyard. One drop of this liquid in the home of the intended victim allegedly triggers the onset of a mysterious illness.

Sometimes the illness is focused on a specific body part. For example, graveyard dust under a pillow is said to cause throbbing headaches. Those wishing to cause kidney failure perform a spell in which they pour buckets of water around the intended victim's yard, saying out loud that they wish that person to lose control of their kidneys. Other evil spells are cast with the hope of causing rashes from head to foot, chills, or even blistered feet.

Many malevolent boko prefer to drive their enemies insane, and most spells to do so involve using the victim's hair. For this reason, it is believed among voodooists that when a person brushes the hair, the loose hairs should be carefully discarded so they do not fall into the hands of a malefic conjurer. If a person fails to do this, someone wishing to harm him or her can hide the hair in a hole in a hackberry tree

A Haitian mambo holds a skull as she waits for customers. Behind her sit all of the ingredients necessary to mix up a malevolent concoction.

and plug it up. If this is done, the victim will purportedly begin hallucinating and exhibiting other symptoms of madness within days. A more modern curse involves wrapping the victim's hair in aluminum foil and throwing it in a river. This is said to cause someone's sanity to flow away.

Those who wish to employ a lighter, less evil, form of black magic can simply cause confusion, disturbances, and arguments in the victim's life. This is called "crossing" and often involves offensive powders that mix some combination of cayenne pepper, graveyard dust, sulfur, and ammonia. These might have names such as Devil's Dust, War Water, or Crossing Powder and are often sold at voodoo shops. These powders are activated by sprinkling them around a victim's home or business. Perhaps one of the more unusual crossing spells is in a recipe provided by Haskins:

> Get a cat and dog and set them at each other. When their hair bristles, cut some from each and mix it with [sulfur] and cayenne. Sprinkle that mixture

Voodoo dolls like these are used to inflict vicarious harm on enemies. Spells are cast on the doll so as to affect the actual person.

inside the target house and the people therein will soon be fighting 'like cats and dogs'.[80]

Voodoo dolls are also used to prevent success and sow confusion. The procedure is to stuff the name of a victim into a slit in the back of a doll along with cayenne pepper. The doll's hands are sewn together, it is blindfolded, and it is placed in a kneeling position in an out-of-the-way corner. Voodooist believe that as long as the doll remains thus disabled, the enemy will allegedly be unsuccessful in life. If the doll is stabbed with pins or kicked, the victim will purportedly feel pain.

The Soulless Zombies

Whatever harm may be caused by a doll or evil spell pales in comparison to what is considered the ultimate voodoo malevolence: turning dead human beings into living zombies. In Haiti, fear of this practice is widespread and there are various theories about it. To those who believe, a zombie is a dead person whose corpse has been exhumed by a boko and induced to assume humanlike functioning. This is achieved by waving under the corpse's nose a bottle that contains its soul, allegedly obtained through magic immediately after the person's death.

Once reanimated, the corpse is a zombie. According to Jean Kerboull in *Voodoo and Magic Practices*, "he becomes a vegetable, a stupid automaton, and the slave and plaything of his master."[81] Hovering in the region between life and death, the glassy-eyed zombie can walk, talk, eat, and work, but has no memory of the past or understanding of its present condition. Hurston describes the horrors of life as a zombie:

> [His] resurrected body [is] dragged from the vault . . . and set to toiling ceaselessly in the banana fields, working like a beast, unclothed like a beast, and like a brute crouching in some foul den in the few hours

Voodoo Dolls

Dolls or human effigies made of wood, wax, clay, or rags are often associated with voodoo. These might be made to resemble a loa or an intended victim. It is said that the power of a voodoo doll is enhanced if it contains something from the targeted victim's body, such as toenails, hair, sweat, saliva, or urine. Someone with evil intent uses the voodoo doll as a focus for a black magic spell in which malevolent thoughts can be concentrated on the effigy. After this is done, the conjurer may "drown" the doll in a bucket of water, set it on fire, or jab it with knives or needles. This will purportedly cause the victim to drown, be burned, or feel extensive stabbing pain. Some traditional voodooists take issue with negative images of the voodoo doll, however, as Bravenet's "Common Misconceptions About Vodoun" Web site explains:

There are no "Voodoo dolls" used in Dahomean Vodoun. A uniquely American hoodoo phenomenon, and Hollywood stereotype, "voodoo dolls" actually have their current origins/usage from pagan Europe. Originally, known as "poppet dolls" (in early Europe), these dolls were used frequently as part of European folk magic and witchcraft as a form of both beneficent and maleficent magic. In Dahomean Vodoun carved wooden images, known as "Bochio" were used largely for this and other purposes. [The] European "poppet doll" was modified and used in lieu of the wooden carved images employed in Vodoun, to symbolized a person, to protect them from sorcery and witchcraft.

allowed for rest and food. From an educated, intelligent being to an unthinking, unknowing beast. Then there is the helplessness of the situation. Family and friends cannot rescue the victim because they do not know. They think the loved one is sleeping peacefully in his grave. They may motor past the plantation where the Zombie who was once dear to them is held captive often and again and its soulless eyes may have fallen upon them without thought or recognition.[82]

The master feeds his zombie only enough to keep it alive. The food must be unsalted because it is alleged that when a zombie tastes even one grain of salt, it will regain consciousness and flee back to the cemetery from whence it came.

Practitioners of black magic believe the power of voodoo dolls can be augmented by using physical items from the victim.

So great is the fear of zombies that some traditionalist Haitians mutilate their deceased relatives in order to make the corpse useless to heinous houngan. This may be done by stabbing the body through the heart, cutting off its head or limbs, removing its intestines or organs, shooting it with a pistol, or injecting it with poison. Those who carry out this macabre task sometimes do so while wearing a disguise so that the zombie boko will not recognize them and take his revenge for being denied a fresh victim.

Toads, Puffer Fish, and Toxins

Folk legends perpetuate the idea that a boko can raise a corpse. However, a more recent theory postulates that zombies were never dead but instead were drugged with a toxic substance mixed up by a boko. The drug is so paralyzing that it slows the heartbeat, pulse, and breathing of the victim to a near stop. It is said that even an experienced doctor will pronounce the person dead, although the victim remains fully conscious. If this were not horror enough, the victim is then given a funeral and buried by grieving relatives, all the while remaining fully aware of his or her circumstances. Some time later the victim is exhumed by the boko and kept in a zombielike state with drugs. In *The Serpent and the Rainbow*, anthropologist and botanist Wade Davis interviewed Clairvius Narcisse, a man who claimed to have lived through this nightmarish experience:

> Quite incredibly, he recalled remaining conscious throughout his ordeal, and although completely immobilized, he had heard his sister weeping by his deathbed. He remembered his doctor pronouncing him dead. Both at and after his burial, his overall sensation was that of floating above the grave. This was his soul, he claimed, ready to travel on a journey that would be curtailed by the arrival of the [boko]

and his assistants. He could not remember how long he had been in the grave by the time they arrived. He suggested three days. They called his name and the ground opened. He heard drums, a pounding, a vibration, and then the [boko] singing. He could barely see. They grabbed him, and began to beat him with a sisal whip [to bring him back to consciousness]. They tied him with rope and wrapped his body in black cloth. Bound and gagged, he was led away on foot by two men. For half the night they walked north until their party was met by another, which took custody of Narcisse. Traveling by night and hiding out by day, Narcisse was passed from one team to the next until he reached the sugar plantation that would be his home for two years.[83]

Davis believes that Narcisse, like other zombies, was given a drug made of toxic herbs mixed with narcotic substances produced by various animals. One such creature, the cane toad *Bufo marinus*, emits a white viscous venom from a gland on its back. This substance, taken in minute quantities, can cause zombie-like behavior including profuse salivation, twitching, shallow breathing, and temporary paralysis. Another creature used by so-called zombie makers is the fish known as the puffer, or blowfish, which manufactures a nerve toxin, or neurotoxin, that is one of the strongest poisons produced in nature. Knowledgeable chefs can make the puffer edible by removing its poison. However, if the puffer is eaten in its natural state, or is secretly placed in a stew or other dish, those who eat it will experience complete paralysis, decreased blood pressure, weak pulse, and other symptoms similar to those experienced by Narcisse. While most victims die, Davis hypothesizes that malevolent houngan have determined a perfect dose over the centuries that allows them to stun their victims without killing them. By

continuing to administer a small dose of the poison daily, houngan are able to keep the dazed zombies in their unfortunate condition indefinitely.

A third theory about Haitian zombies is plausible in some cases. The medical condition called catatonic schizophrenia is a disease of the mind that causes patients to become incoherent and unresponsive to external stimuli. In addition, the muscles become rigid, and the patient appears to be in a stupor similar to the one ascribed to zombies.

Some traditional voodooists dispute the zombie concept completely. While some might be suffering mental illness, Bravenet's "Common Misconceptions About Vodoun" Web site states:

> There are "zombies" only in Hollywood, but not in . . . Vodoun. The Hollywood version of Vodoun cruelly depicts Vodoun healers . . . and diviners as little more than "mumbo jumbo" talking frauds, cannibals and witchdoctors, whose only goal is to steal the souls of their unsuspecting victims, rendering them helpless, walking zombies in the end. . . . Though there are sorcerers who might attempt such a feat, they are a separate and distinct group from the ancestral religion of Vodoun.[84]

Some scholars think a neurotoxin found in the puffer fish is responsible for the phenomenon of zombiism. The toxin is capable of inducing a deathlike state in victims.

Illness and Sudden Death

People attempt to use voodoo in the service of evil. It is often pointed out, however, that these actions are carried out by people who live in extremely difficult conditions. In Haiti, where murder, starvation, and disease are rampant, it may be simpler to attribute evil to black magic rather than to human nature at its worst. As author Victor Turner explains: "Constant exposure to ugly illness and sudden death, and the need to adapt to them swiftly, have surely contributed to the formation of these ugly and irrational beliefs. Once formed, the beliefs feed back into the social process, generating tensions as often as reflecting them."[85]

Zombies Return to the Cemetery

It is said that a zombie will return to its grave if it tastes even one grain of salt. In *The Magic Island* William A. Seabrook describes a scene that purportedly took place in a Haitian marketplace when some zombies were fed salted pralines:

[As] the *zombies* tasted the salt, they knew that they were dead and made a dreadful outcry and arose and turned their faces toward the mountain. No one dared stop them, for they were corpses walking in the sunlight, and they themselves and all the people knew that they were corpses. And they disappeared toward the mountain.

When later they drew near their own village . . . the people of their village . . . recognized among them fathers, brothers, wives, and daughters whom they had buried months before. Most of them knew at once the truth, that these were zombies who had been dragged

dead from their graves, but others hoped that a blessed miracle had taken place . . . and rushed forward to take them in their arms and welcome them.

But the zombies shuffled through the marketplace, recognizing neither father nor wife nor mother, and as they turned leftward up the path leading to the graveyard, a woman whose daughter was in the procession of the dead threw herself screaming before the girl's shuffling feet and begged her to stay; but the grave-cold feet of the daughter and the feet of the other dead shuffled over her and onward; and as they approached the graveyard, they began to shuffle faster and rushed among the graves, and each before his own empty grave began clawing at the stones and earth to enter it again; and as their cold hands touched the earth of their own graves, they fell and lay there, rotting carrion.

Whether used for evil or good, solace or malice, voodoo has had a long history. Today, believers in the United States and elsewhere pick and choose among voodoo beliefs, mainly focusing on the more positive aspects in hopes of improving their lives. For those who continue to practice the dark arts, it is generally acknowledged that they themselves will be punished in the end. Either their spells will be discovered by a houngan who will turn the evil back onto the conjurer, or the victim's family will respond with violence. And true believers in voodoo say that the all-seeing supreme deity Gran Mèt does not condone black magic and can respond with hellish torments. This is a risk that only those with extreme hatred in their hearts will take.

A family of Haitians offers food to dead relatives on New Year's Day, hoping the dead will grant their wishes.

Notes

Introduction: The Many Sides of Voodoo

1. Milo Rigaud, *Secrets of Voodoo*. San Francisco: City Lights, 1985, p. 8.
2. Quoted in Selden Rodman, *Haiti: The Black Republic*. Old Greenwich, CT: Devin-Adair, 1978, p. 61.
3. Phyllis Galembo, *Vodou*. Berkeley, CA: Ten Speed, 1998, p. 78.
4. Samuel H. Williams, *Voodoo Roads*. Wien, Germany: Verlag für Jugend und Volk, 1949, p. 15.

Chapter 1: Historic Roots

5. Ron Bodin, *Voodoo Past and Present*. Lafayette: University of Southwestern Louisiana Press, 1990, p. 5.
6. Jim Haskins, *Voodoo and Hoodoo*. New York: Stein &; Day, 1978, p. 29.
7. Bodin, *Voodoo Past and Present*, p. 7.
8. Alfred Métraux, *Voodoo in Haiti*. New York: Schocken, 1972, p. 30.
9. Quoted in Métraux, *Voodoo in Haiti*, p. 32.
10. M.L.E. Moreau de Saint-Mery, *A Civilization That Perished: The Last Years of White Colonial Rule in Haiti*. New York: University Press of America, 1985, p. 1.
11. Moreau de Saint-Mery, *A Civilization That Perished*, p. 1.
12. Moreau de Saint-Mery, *A Civilization That Perished*, p. 3.
13. Moreau de Saint-Mery, *A Civilization That Perished*, pp. 6–7.
14. Quoted in Métraux, *Voodoo in Haiti*, p. 33.
15. Jim Haskins, *Voodoo and Hoodoo*, p. 52.
16. Quoted in Métraux, *Voodoo in Haiti*, pp. 34–35.
17. Quoted in Leslie G. Desmangles, *The Faces of the Gods*. Chapel Hill: University of North Carolina Press, 1992, p. 27.
18. Rigaud, *Secrets of Voodoo*, p. 13.
19. Quoted in Métraux, *Voodoo in Haiti*, p. 42.
20. Quoted in Métraux, *Voodoo in Haiti*, p. 41.
21. Métraux, *Voodoo in Haiti*, p. 40.
22. Robert Tallant, *Voodoo in New Orleans*. Gretna, LA: Pelican, 1994, p. 19.
23. Tallant, *Voodoo in New Orleans*, p. 12.
24. Tallant, *Voodoo in New Orleans*, p. 34.
25. Lindsey Tubbs and Esther Liu, "Marie Laveau," Voodoo in New Orleans. http://studentweb.tulane.edu/~ltubbs/index.html.
26. Jim Haskins, *Voodoo and Hoodoo*, p. 59.
27. Quoted in Tallant, *Voodoo in New Orleans*, p. 57.

Chapter 2: Houngan, Mambos, and Rituals

28. Moreau de Saint-Mery, *A Civilization That Perished*, p. 1.
29. Moreau de Saint-Mery, *A Civilization That Perished*, pp. 3–4.
30. Quoted in Mêtraux, *Voodoo in Haiti*, p. 36.
31. Moreau de Saint-Mery, *A Civilization That Perished*, p. 4.
32. Mêtraux, *Voodoo in Haiti*, p. 38.
33. Galembo, *Vodou*, p. 78.
34. Rigaud, *Secrets of Voodoo*, p. 34.
35. Mêtraux, *Voodoo in Haiti*, p. 64.
36. Mêtraux, *Voodoo in Haiti*, pp. 64–65.
37. Rigaud, *Secrets of Voodoo*, p. 34.
38. Maya Deren, *Divine Horsemen: Voodoo Gods of Haiti*. New York: Chelsea House, 1970, p. 181.
39. Deren, *Divine Horsemen*, p. 249.
40. Deren, *Divine Horsemen*, p. 30.
41. Deren, *Divine Horsemen*, p. 252.
42. Deren, *Divine Horsemen*, p. 249.
43. Katherine Dunham, *Dances of Haiti*. Los Angeles: Regents of the University of California, 1983, p. 51.
44. Lois Wilcken, *The Drums of Voodoo*. Tempe, AZ: White Cliffs Media, 1992, p. 26.
45. William Sargant, *The Mind Possessed*. Philadelphia: J.B. Lippincott, 1974, p. 181.

Chapter 3: Gods of Voodoo

46. Quoted in Mêtraux, *Voodoo in Haiti*, p. 95.
47. Quoted in Galembo, *Vodou*, p. xx.
48. Zora Neale Hurston, *Tell My Horse*. New York: Harper & Row, 1990, p. 114.
49. Deren, *Divine Horsemen*, pp. 94–95.
50. Desmangles, *The Faces of the Gods*, p. 108.
51. Quoted in Deren, *Divine Horsemen*, p. 98.
52. Desmangles, *The Faces of the Gods*, p. 109.
53. Hurston, *Tell My Horse*, p. 121.
54. Desmangles, *The Faces of the Gods*, p. 125.
55. Quoted in Hurston, *Tell My Horse*, p. 119.
56. Quoted in Deren, *Divine Horsemen*, p. 116.
57. Deren, *Divine Horsemen*, pp. 103–104.
58. Desmangles, *The Faces of the Gods*, p. 115.
59. Deren, *Divine Horsemen*, p. 107.

Chapter 4: Healing and Positive Powers

60. Haskins, *Voodoo and Hoodoo*, p. 140.
61. Ross Heaven, *Voodoo Shaman*. Rochester, VT: Destiny, 2003, pp. 177–78.
62. Heaven, *Voodoo Shaman*, p. 170.
63. Heaven, *Voodoo Shaman*, p. 171.
64. Robert Todd Carroll, "Astral Projection," The Skeptic's Dictionary, 2002. http://skepdic.com/astralpr.html.
65. Quoted in Galembo, *Vodou*, p. 78.
66. Bravenet, "Common Misconceptions About Vodoun," 2004. http://pub47.bravenet.com/faq/show.php?usernum=3951612168&catid=99.
67. Quoted in William A. Seabrook, *The Magic Island*. New York: Harcourt, Brace, 1929, p. 46.

68. Seabrook, *The Magic Island*, p. 47.
69. Seabrook, *The Magic Island*, p. 302.
70. Ray T. Marlbrough, *Charms, Spells and Formulas*. St. Paul, MN: Llewellyn, 1985, pp. 14–15.
71. Marlbrough, *Charms, Spells and Formulas*, p. 131.
72. Haskins, *Voodoo and Hoodoo*, p. 211.
73. Haskins, *Voodoo and Hoodoo*, p. 192.

Chapter 5: Black Magic and Zombies
74. Mêtraux, *Voodoo in Haiti*, p. 268.
75. Haskins, *Voodoo and Hoodoo*, p. 113.
76. Mêtraux, *Voodoo in Haiti*, p. 269.
77. Seabrook, *The Magic Island*, pp. 88–89.
78. Mêtraux, *Voodoo in Haiti*, p. 275.
79. Bart Holland, *What Are the Chances?* Baltimore: Johns Hopkins University Press, 2002, pp. 73–74.
80. Haskins, *Voodoo and Hoodoo*, p. 130.
81. Jean Kerboull, *Voodoo and Magic Practices*. London: Barrie & Jenkins, 1978, p. 67.
82. Hurston, *Tell My Horse*, p. 181.
83. Wade Davis, *The Serpent and the Rainbow*. New York: Simon & Schuster, 1985, p. 62.
84. Bravenet, "Common Misconceptions About Vodoun," 2004. http://pub47. bravenet.com/faq/show.php?usernum =3951612168&catid=104.
85. Quoted in Haskins, *Voodoo and Hoodoo*, p. 115.

For Further Reading

Books

Aloysius M. Lugira, *African Religion*. New York: Facts on File, 1999. Provides a history of African religion and its basic beliefs, discussing oral tradition, ideas of the Supreme Being, rites and rituals, sacred spaces and places, and mystical forces.

Selden Rodman and Carole Cleaver, *Spirits of the Night: The Vaudun Gods of Haiti*. Dallas: Spring, 1992. A book that focuses on the loa of voodoo with chapters on voodoo art, black magic, and ceremony.

Tamara L. Roleff, ed., *Black Magic and Witches*. San Diego: Greenhaven, 2003. Explores the validity of magic and witchcraft with opinions on various sides of the question of whether or not witchcraft is destructive.

Ellyn Sanna, *Folk Religion*. Broomall, PA: Mason Crest, 2003. An exploration of North American folklore traditions, including a chapter on charms and magic, conjurers and healers.

Emily Wade Will, *Haiti*. San Diego: Lucent, 2001. A study of Haiti and its people, culture, and history, including the prevalence of voodoo in that troubled nation.

Web Sites

Bravenet, "Common Misconceptions About Vodoun," 2004. http://pub47.bravenet.com /faq/show.php?usernum=3951612168& catid=99. A Web site dedicated to Dahomean voodoo that dispels negative aspects of voodoo stereotypes perpetuated in movies, books, and the media.

Monstrous.com, "Voodoo Zombies," 2003. http://zombies.monstrous.com/index.htm. A Web site dedicated to several types of zombies with links to articles that describe the origin of zombies and their alleged powers, voodoo zombies, and Hollywood zombies.

Parascope, "The Voodoo Queen, Marie Laveau and New Orleans." www.parascope.com/en /articles/voodooQueen01.htm. A site with historic information about voodoo in New Orleans featuring the queen of voodoo who was at the center of the nineteenth-century movement.

Works Consulted

Ron Bodin, *Voodoo Past and Present*. Lafayette: University of Southwestern Louisiana Press, 1990. A concise work that details voodoo history and practice, especially in Louisiana, with old sensationalistic newspaper accounts of voodoo practices and an interview with a voodoo priestess.

Rod Davis, *American Voudou: Journey into a Hidden World*. Denton: University of North Texas Press, 1998. A journalistic account of travels through the American South where the author participated in various voodoo rituals and ceremonies.

Wade Davis, *The Serpent and the Rainbow*. New York: Simon & Schuster, 1985. A book that puts forth the controversial view that voodoo zombies are a result of deliberate poisoning with toxic substances removed from puffer fish.

Maya Deren, *Divine Horsemen: Voodoo Gods of Haiti*. New York: Chelsea House, 1970. First published in 1953, this book is a classic study of voodoo with a focus on the loa of Haiti, their symbolism, and their relation to the gods of Africa and the saints of Roman Catholicism.

Leslie G. Desmangles, *The Faces of the Gods*. Chapel Hill: University of North Carolina Press, 1992. An examination of the close relationship between voodoo and Roman Catholicism with a focus on the syncretic blend of rituals and mythology.

Katherine Dunham, *Dances of Haiti*. Los Angeles: Regents of the University of California, 1983. A study of the dances used in voodoo ceremonies and other events in Haiti written by an anthropologist who explores the use of dance in order to define ethnological origins.

Phyllis Galembo, *Vodou*. Berkeley, CA: Ten Speed, 1998. This book features dozens of remarkable color photographs of Haitian voodooists and is accompanied by a well-written text by various authors that explains voodoo people and practices.

Jim Haskins, *Voodoo and Hoodoo*. New York: Stein & Day, 1978. A study of Haitian voodoo and its American cousin, hoodoo, as it is practiced by its believers.

Ross Heaven, *Voodoo Shaman*. Rochester, VT: Destiny, 2003. A book written by a voodoo initiate that provides hands-on experience to those who may wish to attempt healing using traditional voodoo techniques combined with shamanic teachings and New Age spirituality.

Bart Holland, *What Are the Chances?* Baltimore: Johns Hopkins University Press, 2002. A book about probability and chance as it relates to superstition and unpredictable events in life such as illness.

Zora Neale Hurston, *Tell My Horse*. New York: Harper & Row, 1990. First published in 1937, this book about the mysteries of voodoo life in Jamaica and Haiti was written by a novelist, folklorist, and anthropologist who was one of the premier African American writers of the Harlem Renaissance in the 1920s.

Jean Kerboull, *Voodoo and Magic Practices*. London: Barrie & Jenkins, 1978. A sensationalistic study of the darker side of voodoo with chapters on ghosts, werewolves, flying witches, and Satanism.

Tanya Krzywinska, *A Skin for Dancing In: Possession, Witchcraft and Voodoo in Film*. Wiltshire, England: Flick, 2000. A study of occult in the cinema with analysis of movies about voodoo comparing content on the screen with the reality as practiced in Haiti.

Michel S. Laguerre, *Voodoo Heritage*. Beverly Hills, CA: Sage, 1980. A discourse on the meaning of voodoo based on ceremonial songs and poems transcribed, studied, and interpreted by the author over a period of several years.

Ray T. Marlbrough, *Charms, Spells and Formulas*. St. Paul, MN: Llewellyn, 1985. A guide to casting spells with instructions on making a gris-gris bag, herb candles, doll magic, incense, oils, and powders, written by a New Orleans hoodoo doctor.

Alfred Métraux, *Voodoo in Haiti*. New York: Schocken, 1972. First published by the anthropologist author in 1959, this comprehensive work explains voodoo rituals, gods, holidays, music, and the religion's relation to Roman Catholicism.

M.L.E. Moreau de Saint-Mery, *A Civilization That Perished: The Last Years of White Colonial Rule in Haiti*. New York: University Press of America, 1985. First published in 1797, this book contains one of the earliest descriptions of a voodoo ceremony along with historical facts about Saint-Domingue before the slave revolution evicted the French.

Robert W. Pelton, *Voodoo Secrets from A to Z*. South Brunswick, NJ: A.S. Barnes, 1973. A comprehensive lexicon of voodoo terms from *ablution* to *zombie* whose language gives great insight into the meaning and substance of voodoo.

Milo Rigaud, *Secrets of Voodoo*. San Francisco: City Lights, 1985. First published in France in 1953 and written by a Haitian author, this book traces the development of voodoo from its African roots to Haiti and the Americas, and reveals the meaning of symbols, signs, rituals, and ceremonies.

Selden Rodman, *Haiti: The Black Republic*. Old Greenwich, CT: Devin-Adair, 1978. A general history of and guidebook to Haiti with chapters on voodoo, the French rule, the independence movement, and Haiti in modern times.

William Sargant, *The Mind Possessed.* Philadelphia: J.B. Lippincott, 1974. A scientific, cultural, and historical examination of spirit possession, mysticism, and faith healing.

William A. Seabrook, *The Magic Island.* New York: Harcourt, Brace, 1929. An eyewitness account of Haitian voodoo in the late 1920s that includes zombies, black magic, and evil sorcery, since discounted by anthropologists as sensationalized and biased.

Robert Tallant, *Voodoo in New Orleans.* Gretna, LA: Pelican, 1994. First published in 1946, this book provides a straightforward picture of voodoo in New Orleans from the eighteenth century to recent times.

Martha Ward, *Voodoo Queen: The Spirited Lives of Marie Laveau.* Jackson: University of Mississippi Press, 2004. A colorful look at the mysterious life of a New Orleans legend who is credited with popularizing voodoo in the nineteenth century.

Lois Wilcken, *The Drums of Voodoo.* Tempe, AZ: White Cliffs Media, 1992. A presentation and analysis of the role drums and drummers play in voodoo rites and ceremonies in Haiti, New York, and elsewhere where voodoo is practiced.

Samuel H. Williams, *Voodoo Roads.* Wien, Germany: Verlag für Jugend und Volk, 1949. The experiences of a college professor whose travels throughout Haiti allowed him to witness voodoo rituals and ceremonies.

Internet Sources

Robert Todd Carroll, "Astral Projection," The Skeptic's Dictionary, 2002. http://skepdic.com/astralpr.html.

Lindsey Tubbs and Esther Liu, "Marie Laveau," Voodoo in New Orleans. http://studentweb.tulane.edu/~ltubbs/index.html.

Index

Picture Credits

About the Author

Stuart A. Kallen is the author of more than two hundred nonfiction books for children and young adults. He has written on topics ranging from the theory of relativity to the history of rock and roll. In addition, Mr. Kallen has written award-winning children's videos and television scripts. In his spare time, he is a singer/songwriter/guitarist in San Diego, California.